THEN FELL THE LORD'S FIRE:
New Life In Ministry

THEN FELL THE LORD'S FIRE:
New Life In Ministry

ORDINATION SERMONS AND ESSAYS ON
PASTORAL THEOLOGY AND PRACTICE

TRANSLATED BY **BROR ERICKSON**

—

BO GIERTZ

2ND EDITION

Then Fell the Lord's Fire: New Life in Ministry. Ordination Sermons and Essays on Pastoral Theology and Practice
© Second Edition, 2025 New Reformation Publications

All rights reserved. No part of this publication may be reproduced, distributed, or transmitted in any form or by any means, including photocopying, recording, or other electronic or mechanical methods, without the prior written permission of the publisher, except in the case of brief quotations embodied in critical reviews and certain other noncommercial uses permitted by copyright law. For permission requests, write to the publisher at the address below.

Scripture quotations marked (ESV) are from The ESV® Bible (The Holy Bible, English Standard Version®), copyright © 2001 by Crossway, a publishing ministry of Good News Publishers. Used by permission. All rights reserved.

All other Scripture references are the author's and translator's translations. Divine pronouns have been capitalized throughout, except in the ESV quotations.

Published by:
1517 Academic, an imprint of 1517.
PO Box 54032
Irvine, CA 92619-4032

Publisher's Cataloging-In-Publication Data
(Prepared by Cassidy Cataloguing Services)

Names: Giertz, Bo, 1905-1998, author. | Erickson, Bror, translator.
Title: Then fell the Lord's fire : new life in ministry : ordination sermons and essays on pastoral theology and practice / Bo Giertz ; translated by Bror Erickson.
Other titles: Då föll Herrens eld. English
Description: Second edition. | Irvine, CA : 1517 Academic, an imprint of 1517, [2026] | Translation of: Då föll Herrens eld. Göteborg : Församlingsförlaget, 1996. | Includes bibliographical references.
Identifiers: ISBN: 978-1-964419-20-6 (paperback) | 978-1-964419-21-3 (ebook)
Subjects: LCSH: Giertz, Bo, 1905-1998—Sermons. | Pastoral theology. | Lutheran Church—Sermons. | Sermons, Swedish—Translations into English. | Ordination sermons. | Church work. | LCGFT: Sermons. | Essays. | BISAC: RELIGION / Sermons / Christian. | RELIGION / Christian Ministry / Pastoral Resources. | RELIGION / Christianity / Lutheran.
Classification: LCC: BX8066.G53 D313 2026 | DDC: 253—dc23

Printed in the United States of America.

Cover art by Zacharaiah James Stuef.

To my dad, John Erickson, a father, pastor, and mentor, who first introduced me to the work of Bo Giertz.

CONTENTS

Foreword ix
Translator's Preface xi

Sermons

Then Fell the Lord's Fire, 1 Kings 18:38 3
Let Not Those Who Hope in You Be Put to Shame through Me,
    Psalm 69:6 6
Let Us Rise Up and Build, Nehemiah 2:17-18 9
The Word Seeks the Lost, Ezekiel 34:16 12
Grant Your Servants to Speak with Boldness, Acts 4:29 15
Do Not Call Any Person Common or Unclean, Acts 10:28 18
Do Everything in the Name of the Lord Jesus, Colossians 3:17 ... 21
You Are My King, Psalm 44:3-4 24
All Shall Be Fulfilled, Luke 18:31 27
I Shall Gladly Offer Myself, 2 Corinthians 12:15 30
Be Not Dismayed, for I Am Your God, Isaiah 41:10 33
His Faithfulness Is a Shield and Buckler, Psalm 91:4 36
On Christ's Behalf, 2 Corinthians 5:20 39
The Gospel, the Power of God, Romans 1:16 42
I Have Called You by Name, Isaiah 43:1 45

The Messenger Is Not Greater than He Who Sent Him,
  John 13:16 47
We Have Received This Ministry by the Mercy of God,
  2 Corinthians 4:1..50
Give Me Your Heart, Proverbs 23:26...........................53
We Live with Him by His Power, 2 Corinthians 13:4............56
You Are My Witnesses, Isaiah 43:12 59
I Received Mercy, 1 Timothy 1:16 62
I Proclaim to You What You Worship as Unknown, Acts 17:23....65
Out of Egypt, Matthew 2:15...................................68
I Bow My Knees before the Father, Ephesians 3:14-15..........71
The Lord Comes to Give You Understanding in Everything,
  2 Timothy 2:7 74
I Am Sending the Promise of My Father upon You, Luke 24:49...77
At Your Word I Will Let Down the Nets, Luke 5:5..............80
My Witnesses in This World, Isaiah 43:12 83

Essays

How the *Seelsorger* Cares for His Own Soul 87
Belief and False-Belief.......................................95
Love Your Brother 102
The Church's Way Today 110
With All Boldness..120
To Preach Justification by Faith 129
The Message from the Unknown 138
Shepherds, Not Lords...147
The Bible's View and the View of the Bible 157
To Believe as the Apostles 166

FOREWORD

Then Fell the Lord's Fire is perhaps a rather wooden translation of the original Swedish title to this book. However, I thought it sounded a bit more poetic than "Then the fire of God came down." So I left it. Truth is, I wanted the whole translation of the first edition to be a bit more wooden in nature. I wanted it to be intelligible in English, but I wanted to keep as much of the original syntax as possible so the reader would occasionally stumble, pause and think about the words they were reading. It's a problem for me that I often read faster than I absorb. I like reading foreign languages because it makes me stop and think a bit more. Early in the morning reading the Greek for Sunday's upcoming pericopes has the same effect. Yet I have repented of this a bit and changed my philosophy of translation a bit over the years. Not everyone enjoys syntactical disruptions in their reading. So when I heard that 1517 wanted to make a new edition of the book I took the opportunity to read through it and give it another layer of polish as well as correct a few typos that somehow always escape attention until the book is on the shelf waiting to be sold.

    This book was first published in Sweden two years before Bo Giertz's death. Since its translation in 2012, it has become a bit of a cult classic among pastors. I found this out as the first edition was yanked from publication, and I started getting phone calls from frantic pastors and friends looking for ordination gifts and encouragement for their brothers in the office. As a bishop in The Gothenburg Diocese of the Church of Sweden from 1949 to 1970, Bo Giertz understood the trials of the office he was ordaining men into. He never shied away from addressing the hardships straight on, and yet his joy in the office never faded. He found strength for the task from God's word, sometimes in the most unlikely of passages. I hope this new edition will continue to help those the Lord has called to serve in the pastoral office that they may not take their hand from the plow, and continue to scatter the seed, water where necessary, and look forward to enjoying the heavenly harvest.

Your Brother in Christ,
Pastor Bror Erickson

TRANSLATOR'S PREFACE

En själasörjar, or as the word has come into use within English-speaking Lutheran circles from German, a *seelsorger*, describes the sainted Bishop Bo Giertz. He was more than a *seelsorger*; he was what his office of bishop demanded he be, a *seelsorger*'s *seelsorger*. The word roughly translated would be a soul worrier, one who worries over souls. There is no good English equivalent. The closest it comes is the antiquated "curate." If one thing could be said of Bo Giertz, it is this: he cared for souls. And he cared for the souls of pastors, especially the cadre in his diocese, and in caring for them, he cared for the people of his diocese.

His bishopric was not an easy one. He had only wanted to be a parish pastor. His memoirs paint his days at the small country parish of Torpa as being some of the happiest years in his career. He enjoyed this work and took it seriously. But a man of his capabilities could not be left alone to study and write and care for a small parish. His book, known in English as *The Hammer of God*, catapulted his popularity with the people, and he was elected bishop. He never stopped being a pastor, never stopped being a *seelsorger*. He never gave up his commitment to God's Word and the Lutheran Confessions. This made it a bit hard for him as bishop when the Church of Sweden chose to ordain women. He knew this compromise his beloved Church of Sweden made with God's Word was just that, a compromise to be followed by more. It was a choice to let culture rather than God's Word determine right and wrong. Bo Giertz never compromised as the Church of Sweden did. He stood firm with God's Word and the Lutheran Confessions. He paid dearly for his convictions, but he remained steadfast, and though his reputation was routinely smeared in the press, his heart never hardened to stone but remained a heart of flesh. He kept his pastoral bearings; he remained anchored in the Word.

For this, he is still loved in Sweden and abroad. I've had the pleasure of knowing a few who served in his diocese when he was bishop and who had the honor to be in his cadre of confessional curates. They have nothing but love and respect for him. To this day, the people of Sweden remember him as the most influential Swedish theologian of the twentieth century. That is no small thing when one considers the names of other Swedish theologians in the twentieth century: Gustaf Aulen, Anders Nygren, Gustaf Wingren, and Bengt Hägglund, to name but a few. Noticeably, most of these men served in academia. The bishops of the twentieth century are largely forgotten, with perhaps the exception of Bishop Söderblom. Many of them were infamous in their day, celebrated as radical, in large part following the antics of Pike and Spong, who, like them, will be forgotten by the world they loved at the expense of the Church, seeking power and opportunity and using it for self-aggrandizement. But not Bishop Giertz. With every passing year, his influence grows wider, his memory more cherished as the Church remembers and honors her heroes.

As his influence grows wider, it is a curious thing that so little of his work is known in English, and this despite their wide popularity and translations into even obscure languages such as Zulu. *The Hammer of God* is celebrated by many, but it is almost all that is known of his works, and until quite recently was missing whole chapters in English translation. A precious few others, such as *Liturgy and Spiritual Awakening*, were ever translated to English and those too in piecemeal fashion. Only recently has that begun to change, as his devotional *To Live with Christ* has become available, followed by his novel *The Knights of Rhodes* and his more dogmatic book Christ's Church, translated by my friend Hans Andrae.

This collection of ordination addresses and essays on pastoral theology and practice first found publication in Norway, where due to its proximity to Sweden, the bishop has many admirers. As the book gained popularity there, demand grew for it to be published in Sweden also. Permissions were gained, and the book was published in Sweden in 1996, two years before the bishop's death, by the Församlingsförlaget in Gothenburg, with help from Samfundet Pro Fide et Christianismo ock Stiftelsen Bo Giertz's 90 årsfund to offset the cost of publication. It must be said that these organizations have given the world of Lutheranism an incredible gift. There are some books that just demand to be translated, and this is one. Those who have helped me with this project, Brigitte Mueller, Peggy Pedersen, Donovan Riley, Eric Andrae, Wade Johnston, and Jonathan Schkade, need also be thanked for their work and support in this project. We are also thankful to the Giertz estate for granting permission for this important and needed book to be published in English. Here in these pages, the bishop's crosier continues his work of caring for his Church and her pastors. In a day when burnout and fatigue are so common among even seasoned pastors and young pastors encounter early disillusionment, this book brings healing and comfort for the *seelsorger*'s soul and truly practical advice. Here, the Lord's fire falls to kindle new joy and new resolve in the life of the Lord's servants. Here, a pastor will find Law and Gospel applied to him. Here, a pastor will find the bread he needs to sustain himself in his work. Many pastors are known to read The Hammer of God on a yearly basis; many will find these sermons worth the same devotion. I know I have.

Your brother in Christ, Bror Erickson
Monday after Trinity Sunday

SERMONS

Ordination Sermon 1952

THEN FELL THE LORD'S FIRE,
I Kings 18:38

Then the fire of the LORD fell and consumed the burnt offering and the wood and the stones and the dust, and licked up the water that was in the trench.
—1 Kings 18:38 ESV

We are reminded of the story of the duel on Mt. Carmel between Elijah and the prophets of Baal. All day long, the prophets of Baal limped around their altar and cried out loudly while cutting themselves with swords and spears. But not a sound was heard, and no one answered. Then Elijah stepped forward and rebuilt the Lord's altar that had been thrown down, laid the wood and the sacrifice upon it, and let water be poured over it. Then, when the time was right for the burnt offering, he called to God and said:

> "Answer me, O LORD, answer me, that this people may know that you, O LORD, are God, and that you have turned their hearts back." Then the fire of the LORD fell and consumed the burnt offering and the wood and the stones and the dust, and licked up the water that was in the trench (1 Kgs. 18:37-38 ESV).

Every true pastor has prayed like Elijah many times. He has prayed thus when he would step before the people with the Lord's Word. He has prayed thus when he fought with the powers of unbelief and opposing indifference and the darkness of false belief in his own heart: "Answer me, O LORD, answer me, that this people may know that you, O LORD, are God, and that you have turned their hearts back." Perhaps then the Lord answered with fire from heaven, as on the first Pentecost or in the days when He sent the wind of revival over our fathers. These are the greatest days of God's Church, her days of harvest and days of celebration when the Lord's fire falls from heaven.

Every young pastor wishes and prays that he would see at least a little of this. If he goes out to serve with an upright heart, then he will go out with some of Elijah's spirit and power to turn the children's hearts to their fathers and teach them to love the Church of their fathers and their fathers' faith. He longs to build up the Lord's broken-down altar. He will cry to the halfhearted, "How long will you limp on both sides?" He will step forward from Mt. Carmel and refute the prophets of unbelief, even if he stands there alone. But most of all, he wants to see the fire fall, see new hearts kindled, see the sinners consumed by the fire of Golgotha's sacrifice and the flame of faith so clear against the sky, and hear it as a repentant, trembling, yet victory-sure confession of the congregation: "The Lord is He who is God!"

This is not romanticism. A young pastor must think, pray, and hope this way if he believes in his Lord, in His Word, and trusts in His promises. Yet there is something else that belongs to this privilege of going with the spirit and power of Elijah, something that a servant of the Lord can learn through humiliation and setbacks while he waits for the fire that will fall from heaven. It so seldom happens that the Lord straightens the way to Mt. Carmel's top for His servants and lets him who answered in prayer see the fire fall from heaven. This was also true for Elijah. Before the fire fell on Mt. Carmel, he had to fight through long years of persecution and loneliness. There was the time of great drought. There were the lonely nights in the cave by the brook Cherith. There were the days of a refugee, when he had to live from hand to mouth every day by a miracle of God. And then the fire fell. It wasn't the end of persecution and murder. Lonely and bitter, he sat under a broom tree in the desert of Beer-Sheba: "It is enough; now, O LORD, take away my life" (1 Kgs. 19:4 ESV). And the great prophet was again allowed to be rebuked and reared like an un-understanding and grumbling boy. He was able to start over from the beginning in his Lord's service. Yet under his Lord's discipline, he was, in the end, the greatest teacher in Israel, a father of his people, worth more than both chariots and riders.

Beloved young brothers, you who stand here today to be ordained to the holy pastoral office! If it is your prayer and your longing to see the Lord's fire fall from heaven and have a little of it light your own heart, then Elijah's story will come alive again in you. In different ways and through various experiences, God comes to carry out the work that He does with every true pastor who longs for the Lord's fire. God testifies to such a pastor. He does it first and foremost by keeping him under His discipline. There is so much that must be pruned by the vineyard keeper's knife. Maybe it happens during a time of great drought when all seems to be fizzling out in the congregation. The pastor knows that it is an affliction from the Lord, a punishment for an apostate generation. But he may himself trust that all the more and bear the weight of the burden, all the while standing there as the Lord's witness and exhorting repentance. Maybe it happens during severe persecution or great loneliness when the Lord's pusillanimous servant says with Elijah, "They have torn down Your altars. They have betrayed Your covenant. I alone am left." And for the same reproving answer: "I have left seven thousand men who have not bowed their knee to Baal." Maybe it needs to go as it did on Mount Horeb. Storm and earthquake and fire pass by, but the Lord was not in this. Perhaps the pastor must first learn that noise and commotion, altercation and sensation, influx of people, and human conscientiousness does not mean revival. The fire that seemed to flare up was not the Spirit's true fire. Perhaps it was only manmade feelings and such movement as man can bring about with human eloquence. But then comes a soft whisper, and then it was the Lord.

Until the end, the Lord's fire falls. Maybe not so that it flares and burns in the whole congregation. It may only be a little here and a little there, individual people who wake up, worried souls that open themselves, new communicants who dare come to the Lord's Table and remain there. If God's servant stands the test, if he stays as a witness—even if he thinks he stands alone—if he patiently suffers persecution and disgrace, if he lets himself be disciplined and straightened out, if he continues to sow the Word faithfully and honestly, then he shall also see the Lord's fire fall from heaven, maybe where he least expected it. For his gifts of grace and his calling are from God. He cannot repent of either the gifts of grace or the calling he bestows upon you today, who will now be ordained to the holy pastoral office. For so says the Lord: Go out where I send you, and then speak what I ask you. Fear not for them, for I am with you and will help you. And it is the Lord who is God. Yes, the Lord is God. Amen.

Ordination Sermon for May 19, 1953

LET NOT THOSE WHO HOPE IN YOU BE PUT TO SHAME THROUGH ME,
Psalm 69:6

Let not those who hope in you be put to shame through me,
O Lord God of hosts;
let not those who seek you be brought to dishonor through me,
O God of Israel.

—Psalm 69:6 ESV

1. This prayer of King David is a good prayer for a pastor, a necessary prayer that needs to be prayed often.

The worst that can happen to a pastor is not that he himself comes to shame, that he fails, or is never appreciated as a preacher or promoted more than those ordained with him. Many for whom it has so gone have been good stewards of their gifts and, in the end, were received by their Lord with joy. No, the worst that can happen with a pastor is this: on account of him, those who put their trust in God are put to shame, and those who expected something else of their pastor left for good in their disappointment. Maybe they never really had any true faith, but they had been awakened and began to ask about God, confused and groping, as newly awakened men do. Or possibly they had a restless longing for faith ever since childhood. They listened and hoped that something would happen, something that made them certain that there was a God, certain that Jesus was God's Son and their Savior.

And they came to shame because of their pastor. Maybe his preaching was too empty and worthless, too ill-prepared and without guidance.

Or possibly because his life was so glaringly contrary to the Gospel he proclaimed. With the seeking fear of unbelief, they sought that which was genuine, that which could bear fruit of the Spirit, that which would show that Christ can take up residence in the heart of man. Instead, they find self-centeredness, lust for money, gossiping, and concern for one's own fame. So they came to shame. They hoped in God, they wanted to see Jesus, and they found nothing other than the same self-love, the same hankering for money and fame that they knew all too well before. They turn away with bitterness. Maybe they become hard and cynical. They seem to see fraud in all of Christendom. That is the worst that can happen to a pastor.

2. Therefore, this is a necessary prayer for a pastor, a prayer that he needs to pray often: "Let not those who hope in you be put to shame through me, O Lord GOD of hosts."

It is a prayer in temptation, maybe the last straw to grab onto in the most extreme and hardest of temptations. Even if it has gone so long that the pastor, during a day of evil, is ready to give it all up, even if he thinks that he can do the same with himself, that he is nothing more than a lost sinner who may as well just give up the fight, even then this remains clear: there are others—those who wait upon God, those who would possibly lose all the ground under their feet, if something like that happened to their pastor, their confirmation teacher, he who taught them to seek God and recognize spiritual realities. It is necessary for a pastor to think about them in the evil days. Even if in his despair he thinks it makes no difference what happens to him, he cannot think that way of the others, the youth, the parishioners, and the many asking and waiting who seek their Lord. He cannot let them come to shame. He grabs hold of God's hand anew and prays, "Let not those who hope in you be put to shame through me, O Lord GOD of hosts."

It is also a prayer for every day, in success and joy. There are so many hidden temptations, not the least in that which seems good and gives the pastor mere fame. The more the pastor is a *seelsorger* and instructor, the more he needs to be ready for man's awakening and conversion, the more he notices that the Word is being received, the more seriously he needs to pray, "Let not those who hope in you be put to shame through me, O Lord GOD of hosts." It is so easy to slack in watchfulness. It is so easy to be spoilt. It is so quickly done when the opponent unexpectedly rears up to let his old Adam join the fight. It seems so natural to try to cover up one's tracks after a blunder or to hide a mistake. But in just this small thing lies the beginning for the sins through which we can bring the asking hopefuls to shame. Therefore, the pastor needs to pray, also in everyday humdrum and success: "Let not those who seek you be brought to dishonor through me, O God of Israel."

3. Many pastors have prayed this same prayer in times of *anfechtung* ["existential angst"], maybe as a desperate cry to a silent God who seems to hide His face. The work all seems to be fruitless, the prayer all in vain, all the preaching as if sowing on the path. What has become of God's promise? That which has been so certain that the Word would not return empty? The pastor might think that he could bear his own shame, but here, there is the salvation of man. Here it is about God's glory, so he cries out in despair, "How can You, Lord? How can You let them who hope in You come to shame in me?" In this situation, it is necessary for a pastor to read all of Psalm 69. It is itself such a cry of despair to God. But then it says: "O God, you know my folly; the wrongs I have done are not hidden from you" (Ps. 69:5 ESV). With these words, all our accusations end. It is still me who is wrong. I have not served as faithfully as I should. I have not done what He had the right to expect of me. So I may begin to pray again, "Let not those who hope in you be put to shame through me, O Lord GOD of hosts." It is altogether my sin; may the others not suffer because I am such a poor pastor. May Christ have mercy on me. I know that I am the greatest among sinners.

And then I am again at the point where God can begin to work anew, where He makes the weak strong, where He shows His glory through forgiving and justifying undeservedly and without measure.

We who are tested by the call's most difficult blessings today, you who now enter it, we know that these difficulties are also blessings in God's hand. Be it your upright prayer that God shall be glorified and none come to shame through your work, so shall God let all the work of your office, both successes and failures, serve God's glory and bring souls to blessedness.

Ordination Sermon for December 29, 1953

LET US RISE UP AND BUILD,
Nehemiah 2:17-18

Then I said to them, 'You see the trouble we are in, how Jerusalem lies in ruins with its gates burned. Come, let us build the wall of Jerusalem, that we may no longer suffer derision.' And I told them of the hand of my God that had been upon me for good, and also of the words that the king had spoken to me. And they said, 'Let us rise up and build.' So they strengthened their hands for the good work.
—Nehemiah 2:17–18 ESV

When it is narrated like this in the second chapter of Nehemiah, the story applies to us also. Israel and Jerusalem are the forerunners of the Christian Church. In their changing fate, we can always see ourselves anew, as if in a play. The voices from the past begin to speak of our own distress and our own joy.

For those who love our Swedish Church, the picture of Zion laid waste is particularly disturbing. The heart beats when one reads of Nehemiah's nightly ride among the ruins and of his burning desire to do the impossible so that God's city might rise up out of destruction. It is not difficult to perceive that there is a message for us here too, a message that will set our hearts on fire and demand of us to build upon God's command.

God's Swedish Zion lies broken-down before our eyes. At one time, God's Church was built in our land to reveal God's love for all of His people. As a mother, she cared for her children, reached out to them all, understood them, and spoke to them so that they understood that she spoke with God's voice. What was then built is now, in large part, destroyed. Through neglect and misunderstanding, her walls have been allowed to fall. Enemies have burnt her gates, and all too often, she herself has betrayed the cause she should have championed through weak faith and timidity, through laziness, and lack of zeal. She has not been a mother for the many who sought their livelihood in new work at the office and in factories. She did not understand them; she did not seek them and was not able to rightly serve the Lord who wants to gather them also, as a shepherd gathers his sheep and a hen her chicks under her wings. So she all too often fulfilled the Savior's word about the unrepentant city: "See your house is left to you desolate." So has her deficient service been revealed before the world, and today, she bears the shame for much that she did not believe was able to happen within her walls, but which now goes forth and cries out from the roof.

And what shall now be said among those who still care for these walls? What, if not just this: "Let us build up Jerusalem's walls, so that we may no longer suffer derision"?

In the whole of God's Swedish church today, this ought to be a unanimous desire: to build up God's congregation again. Nowhere, ought this desire be more sincere and burning than among those who are ordained into the holy pastoral office. It is precisely through them that God, according to His own word, will "equip the saints for the work of ministry, for building up the body of Christ." How shall God's Jerusalem be built up anew?

It shall be built on the right foundation. Another foundation cannot be laid other than the one that is laid: Jesus Christ. The message shall ring, truthful, paid in full, unadulterated, just as it was given to us once and for all.

It shall be built with the right earnestness. The breaches in the wall can only be healed by penance and repentance. That which was broken down through dishonesty shall be built up in glory and humility. That which was lost through selfishness and haughtiness, it shall be restored through servanthood and unselfishness. That which was destroyed and squandered through inertia and misunderstanding shall be taken back by sacrificial and selfless seeking after souls.

"Let us rise up and build." It was the natural and straightforward answer that Nehemiah received from his appeal. It is the same answer that God's Church today expects of each and every one of us who knows God's hand touches his heart. It is also the promise and the intention that God's Church expects of those who are ordained to the holy ministry: "Let us rise up and build."

Rise up and build. It is the exhortation for the many days of work ahead—particularly for the days when one would like to sit in peace and quiet, when one would like to escape the hard work of building, when one would be satisfied to watch what others have built. So long as God's temple is still broken down, so long as the poor souls who should be living stones in God's house lay strewn as dead blocks in a quarry, so long shall the Lord hear the willing voices of His servants saying, "Let us rise up and build."

They took courage for the good work.[1] This can be needed, that here one takes courage for himself, courage to know his sin, courage to confess his Lord, courage to bear his disgrace, courage to try new methods, courage to hold fast to the old, courage to fail.

Where can one get such courage? Not of himself. Only through the certainty that the work is God's and that one serves the Lord, before whom one daily lays down his sin, confesses his mistakes, receives forgiveness for his negligence, and is clothed with the task to go out again.

It is this task from the Lord that His Church gives to you today as you are now ordained into the pastoral office. We wish you good courage for this good work. The task is not less because the time is hard. It is no smaller task to build up the desecrated Jerusalem than to build there in the good days. It was truly no smaller task to preach before the people of captivity than to be a prophet in the undestroyed Zion. All right, let us rise up and build up Jerusalem's walls, so that we may no longer suffer derision. Yes Lord, we will rise up and build. Amen.

---

[1] The more literal translation from the Swedish is: "So they strengthened their hands for the good work."

Ordination Sermon for May 16, 1954

THE WORD SEEKS THE LOST,
Ezekiel 34:16

I will seek the lost, and I will bring back the strayed,
and I will bind up the injured, and I will strengthen the weak,
and the fat and the strong I will destroy.
I will feed them in justice.
—Ezekiel 34:16 ESV

The Lord does all this through His Word. If this should happen through the service of a pastor, then he must first and foremost see to it that the Word goes out pure and clear.

It is the Word that seeks the lost, that touches the heart of man and lets him know that God seeks after him. But then the Word must be God's Word, the living Word from God's lips that is filled with God's longing for His children. It is the Word that brings back the strayed. Only the Word can show the way home. If the Word is corrupted, it cannot lead right. If our preaching does not lead the way, does not point to the springs of life in the Bible and the Lord's Supper, if it does not speak clearly about the sins that bind men and haul them away, then neither can it lead them back.

It is the Word that binds up the injured. If the preaching cannot paint Christ as crucified and cannot proclaim His atoning death, then neither can it heal the wounded conscience. Then it only leads to patchwork, to complacency, to uncertainty, or to despair.

It is the Word that strengthens the weak. Only a rightly proclaimed Word can show men that in the midst of their weakness they can and may live through faith in Jesus, that it is the faith in Him that makes them children of God, and that it is this faith that strengthens our weakness so that we do not tire of seeking the forgiveness of sins and do not tire of fighting against our Old Adam.

It is the Word that pastors are ordained to bring out honestly, humbly, persistently. If he bargains, and skimps, compromises and blots out, he hinders the Word from seeking, bringing back, binding up, and strengthening.

When the pastor is ordained to carry this Word out into the world, he is consecrated to live and operate as the Word does. As the Word's servant, he must himself go out with the Word to seek and lead back, bind up and strengthen.

He shall seek men out with the Word. It can be said of our Swedish people just the same as God says about Israel in this chapter of Ezekiel: "My sheep were scattered, they wandered over all the mountains and on every high hill." And often it could be added also from this word of Scripture: "With none to search or seek for them" (Ez. 34:6 ESV). It is this that has all too often happened. When one breaks from his old congregation and his habitual life conditions and finds haven in new quarters and new ways of life, there doesn't seem to be anyone to seek or search after him. One demands that he should seek out the church, but the church does not seek him out.

The pastor, who is the bearer of the Word, must do what the Savior did. The Son of Man came to seek the lost. He sought out Matthew at the tax booth and the fishermen at their nets. He found Zacchaeus by the roadside and went to be a guest in his house. He gained a reputation for being good friends with tax collectors and sinners and was found in company where no one expected to find a proclaimer of the Word.

Such is the Word. It is not locked in the sanctuary. It does not ring only at particular hours. It searches for men. That which is given to the servant of the Word bears within itself a running power, the Word's longing for men every day. The Shepherd must seek the lost. The woman searches after her silver coin in every corner. She lights lamps and sweeps where she thinks she may have sat in pleasant peace. So the Word must seek the lost. So the pastor must always drive out to those who will not come to him.

He shall of course bring them back. He shall always seek again to get within earshot of those who have fallen away from the Word. Many times it is like Israel's banished men, men who were driven away from the Word by circumstances that they themselves seemed to have had little control over. They lived in a world where the church seemed to have disappeared. Their home and their surroundings, their work and the everyday world made it the least natural of all that they should go to church. They belonged to the banished. They are like Israel, who in the time of the prophets had been carried away from the temple and settled in a strange land among a people who did not celebrate the Lord's Divine Service. Should these banished be led back, then they must be sought. The pastor must be their friend and their confidant, their servant and their helper, who, with all his being, shows that he loves them and that their well-being lays heavy on his heart.

He shall bind the wounded. He who binds up must often go to the wounded, bend down over him, take him just as he is. It is not enough to sit in his comfortable place and declare himself prepared to bind up those who present themselves to be bound up. The servant of the Word must go out on the roads and paths, search and seek to be a Christ to his neighbor.

He shall strengthen the weak. He shall not place demands of genuineness, nor demand that everything should be just as he wishes it would be. He may count on just that weakness that must be found in the scattered and wounded. He shall not demand strength where there isn't any. He may count on it that there is no knowledge here, no confessionalism, no perseverance, no good church customs. He may speak as to children, have patience as with those who are sick, for he shall be all, so that in all circumstances he shall save some.

To this great task you are consecrated today. The task to proclaim the Word is entrusted to you today. The Word demands all of the man. It shall have control over all of you, over your proclamation, and over your life.

May it live in your preaching so that it becomes a gathering, healing, and strengthening Word. May it live in all of your being so that you yourself become a gatherer who seeks the lost, brings back the scattered, binds up the wounded and strengthens the weak. Amen.

Ordination Sermon for May 25, 1955

GRANT YOUR SERVANTS TO SPEAK WITH BOLDNESS,
Acts 4:29

And now, Lord, look upon their threats and grant to your servants to continue to speak your word with all boldness.
—Acts 4:29 ESV

This prayer originates from the first days of the Christian Church, from the first days of persecution after the first Pentecost. We need to constantly pray this prayer anew in the Christian Church and with particular zeal when we ordain new servants to walk in the holy pastoral office.

The pastoral office was called the preaching office of old. To preach is the pastor's most important task. He is ordained to proclaim God's Word, sent by God Himself with the message that shall go out to all people in all times. The pastor can say with the word of the apostles, "Therefore we are ambassadors for Christ, God making his appeal through us" (2 Cor. 5:20 ESV).

It is not presumptuous that he says this. It would be presumptuous if he built upon his own thoughts and preached his own philosophy or thoughts on life. But it is just this he does not do and will not do. He thinks about Christ. He is a steward charged with a task that he has not taken upon himself. He can say as the apostles, "He commanded us to preach to the people and to testify that he is the one appointed by God to be judge of the living and the dead" (Acts 10:42 ESV).

Preaching is also done in the power of Christ's Word, as Paul says. The pastoral office presupposes faith in Christ and His Word, a childlike, honest, firm, and fearless faith in the Lord Christ, who was sent by

God for our salvation and who spoke the Word that is spirit and life. It is this faith in the Word that God released into the world so that we would learn to know Him and His Son. It is faith that God still speaks to us through this Word. He gave us the Bible just as it is so that the Word would be able to speak at all times and to all people, so that even today He would be able to lead and teach, discipline and comfort whomever will listen to Him.

This boldness also depends on this simple and honest certainty that God speaks through this Word, and it is this Word that I am sent to proclaim as a pastor.

This boldness is needed. It has never been easy to be a proclaimer. If the Word is rightly proclaimed, then it will also awaken offense. All men have made for themselves some picture of God. There is also a revelation outside the Word, in nature and conscience. It is fragmentary and unclear, but it gives to man a diffuse belief in a god and a common morality. When the Gospel is proclaimed, saying that this does not count, men often become indignant. With complete naivety they answer that that part of the revelation that they have encountered up till now is self-evident and reasonable, but the revelation in Christ that now touches them is narrow-minded and uncertain.

The pastor could adapt himself and preach just that which he knows is now current religious truth. Such a proclamation will not awaken any opposition, but neither does it awaken anybody from spiritual slumber. It neither exposes nor comforts. It is neither hot nor cold. It is not God's Word, and so it does not create faith.

Therefore all God's Church needs to pray that the Lord may let His servants proclaim His Word with all boldness, and nothing but His Word. Even more this prayer is needed by those who will be ordained to proclaim this Word themselves.

How can one get such boldness to proclaim the Word as a message from God?

The answer is very simple: by experiencing it as a message from God. If one wants to understand it, if he wants to know if this teaching is from God or if it is man's word, then Jesus says he shall do God's will. Then he shall take the Word seriously, place himself under the Word, apply the Word to himself. The Word shows its truth powerfully when a person lets it into his heart and his life. No one needs it more than the pastor. For him it applies both to his own being and the salvation of others. If he does not let the Word work on him, then all the work of his office becomes false and distorted. His preaching becomes the fearful prater and powerless thoughts of men, or it becomes a caricature of boldness, human conceit that changes the Word into something else, a spiritual bully that doesn't allow himself to be disciplined by God's law. Behind true boldness, there is always humility and mercy. It is found only where a man ever again bows in the confession of sins before the Word's demand and is ever again established by its promise. It is the pastor who needs the Word himself, just as it is written, to be able to live, so that he can also preach it for others as a living Word from God.

Today God's Church prays once again that the Lord may let His servants proclaim His Word with all boldness. We pray it with particular concern for you, who now come to be placed in the great test, the pastor's inevitable test, which shall reveal if he preaches on Christ's behalf as his Lord has commanded him to preach, or if he comes to it with his own thoughts or a skillful reflection of man's desires. May the Lord lead you to live by this Word, to not be able to live without it, and to not to be able to leave it. Then He shall also give you, His servants, grace to proclaim it with all boldness.

Ordination Sermon for December 30, 1956

DO NOT CALL ANY PERSON COMMON OR UNCLEAN,
Acts 10:28

And he said to them, 'You yourselves know how unlawful it is for a Jew to associate with or to visit anyone of another nation, but God has shown me that I should not call any person common or unclean.'
—Acts 10:28 ESV

It is Peter who says this in the company of heathen and foreigners, who, as a faithful Jew, he really should not have gone to see. It was of course God Himself who forbade His people to make alliances with the alien people in the land of Canaan. They were to be consecrated to their God. Alone in the world, this little people would witness to the truth. The flame of truth would not be escaped. Whatever happened, Israel was not allowed to have dealings with the foreign people and their gods.

This commandment of God applied for its time. It was given for the long centuries of preparation and expectation when God fostered His people through the prophets and pushed forward the world's fate against the day of revelation, the day when that which He did in Israel would have meaning for the whole world. When the time was ready, God sent His Son. The Son showed with all of His life that God really did not count any people as unholy or unclean. It was precisely the lost and despised that He sought. He went to sinners, kept company with publicans and harlots, was a guest in Zacchaeus's house where the pious of the city would not dare set foot. Time and time again He amazed His disciples, and His slanderers were again and again given grist for their mill. He ought to know what kind of woman she is! How can He eat with sinners! Was He not a glutton and drunkard, good friends with publicans and sinners!

Yeah, how could He?

Even today it happens that His own have difficulty understanding Him and still more difficulty following Him. It is so easy for us to draw boundaries and let them determine our manner of assessing and treating people.

How could He?

So He does as only the Lord can do, who knows that He must judge all, and who has yet resolved to include all in boundless atonement. So is God. See, no one can trust in his own holiness. Before Him every mouth is stopped and the whole world stands in guilt. And then He determined to atone for all through the Son, since He, with the blood of His cross, prepared peace. That was the price. It cost God that much to be the friend of sinners and to be able to take the unholy up in His holy communion.

He who understands this, he is ready to consider no one as unholy or unclean. We all stand condemned, and yet God still reaches out with His fatherly arms to all. God has taught me this, Peter says. It is easy to understand that it was not easy to learn this. It required the whole witness of Jesus' life and His shocking manner of keeping company with the fallen. It also required Peter's own fall, his denial and perjury, his bitter tears over a failed attempt to be a faithful disciple. Finally, it required the Savior's total forgiveness and His command "Feed my sheep" (John 21:17 ESV). Be a shepherd for My sheep. Peter was now sent out into the world to be a witness to this atonement and this forgiveness. God had taught him to not consider anyone unholy or unclean.

God needs to teach the same thing to His pastors at all times. It is not easy to learn this. On the one hand, one must see that God's Law applies without bargain. The Scriptures have really encompassed all under sin. Sin is not small inoffensive weaknesses. It can be so fearful that the priest time and time again reels back. He may see and hear much that he could hardly believe was possible. He might do it when he listens to man's confessions or may see into a torn home and failed life. He comes to meet many types of evil and slander that he hardly would have been prepared for if he weren't a pastor. Sin is a reality. It shall not be made light of but taken seriously in both preaching and soul care.

So then, the pastor shall not consider any one of these men as unholy or unclean in this meaning so that he considers them hopelessly lost or as men in whom neither God nor His Church have any interest. The earth is the Lord's and all that lives therein. He has created them all.

Every man we meet is created from His hand. They are watched by the Father's eyes and sought by His love. He has baptized most of them. They are His own children that He does not forget. Therefore, the Church is the people's Church, and the pastor is the whole congregation's pastor. The fewer men that know of God's Church, the more the pastor should meet with them in the conviction that God knows of them, that he has a purpose for their lives and will not let them be lost. If God is not in their thoughts, then they are in God's thoughts. When the pastor meets them in this conviction, then he cannot consider any of them unholy or unclean.

When we today ordain new servants of the Word, who shall carry out the holy ministry in God's Church in Sweden, we have reason to rejoice that even our church, through its ordinances and its congregational life shows that she will follow the Lord's command to not consider anyone unholy or unclean. It is great to be a pastor in such a church. It can contain temptation. The mercy that does not condemn can easily become lax tolerance that accepts anything. The pastor is placed to watch that the Word may go out also as a judge of our sins, all sins without consideration of person. Yet at the same time, he is a servant of mercy that has atoned for all and can forgive all. There is one person who the pastor always considers unholy and unclean. It is himself. The more he learns to know his own heart with all of its sluggishness and wretchedness, the more he comes to love his Savior and be struck with wonder that the grace does not run out, that his Lord never tires to forgive, that he is not ashamed to call great sinners brothers, friends, and coworkers. And all the more the pastor comes to love his lost brothers. He who receives much forgiveness, he cannot count any of his wretched fellow men as unholy or unclean.

So we ordain you today to the holy pastoral office and pray that all three of you may be honest servants of the Lord, who encompassed everything together as sin in order to show mercy to all. May His mercy always stay with you. May you always hold the doors of mercy open for those gone astray and lost.

Ordination Sermon for January 5, 1957

DO EVERYTHING IN THE NAME OF THE LORD JESUS,
Colossians 3:17

And whatever you do, in word or deed, do everything in the name of the Lord Jesus, giving thanks to God the Father through him.
—Colossians 3:17 ESV

This exhortation that is meant for all Christians, for all walks of life and for all times, is particularly meant for those who stand before the Lord's altar to be received into the pastoral office. Therefore the first of the five questions that is directed to one becoming a pastor reads thus: "Will you, in God's name, the triune name, take on the holy office of ministry and take pains thereof that you may in all things give God the glory and blessedness to souls?"

One takes the holy pastoral office on himself in God's name, the triune name.

1. This means first and foremost that one is ordained in order to be an instrument of God, to speak in His name, and on His behalf. The task comes from the Lord Himself. It is not a service that man has instituted. It is not only human laws and regulations that belong to this office and how it shall be carried out. The essence comes from God. A pastor shall serve his Lord with hand and mouth. He shall preach the Word as it has been given him. He shall operate at the baptismal font and the Lord's Table as he has been commanded. Therefore the Lord says to His first ambassadors: "He who hears you, hears Me. If you forgive someone his sins they are forgiven." Here also the word of the apostle applies: "therefore we are ambassadors for Christ, God making

His appeal through us." Therefore one must take on this office in the name of the triune God.

2. This means furthermore that he who is ordained to this office must consecrate his will and his power to his Lord's unreserved service. He who takes upon himself this office in God's triune name knows that he is now a steward, a living steward that possesses nothing, not even himself. What the Lord expects of His steward is that he shall be faithful. He has received so much entrusted to him that being unfaithful is doubly serious. He must take pains that this office really gives glory to God and blesses souls. It is the first duty of the office to be faithful—faithful to the Word, the message from God, both when it means to proclaim it to others, and that he applies it to himself, faithful to his Lord's will both when it means to explain it for others, and letting it form his own life.

This is the most hazardous where it means to take upon oneself the pastoral office in God's name—he who dares credit himself to be such a steward, who his Lord can trust in all and who comes to fulfill all that has been commanded of him. No one should dare to take upon himself such a task in the Lord's name, if that name were not also the name of Jesus, the name of God's own Son, who gave Himself to make amends for that which the servants had broken. In His name the forgiveness of sins shall be preached. Whoever believes in Him shall receive the forgiveness of sins in His name. Even the pastor can believe in that promise. To take upon yourself this office in the name of the triune God means to step into the service of a Lord who gave His own life in order to make good all the mistakes and neglect of His servants. To every day receive the forgiveness of sins in Jesus' name also means that every day you undertake to do all you do whether in word or deed in the name of Jesus. For where there is forgiveness, there is the Lord Himself. "In Jesus' name" is not some empty formula that one can write as an excuse for his neglectfulness. In Jesus' name is the Lord Jesus Himself, with all His mercy and righteousness. Therefore the name is really a power that flattens out all guilt and covers up all unrighteousness. Yet for this reason, the name is also a power that cannot leave us unaffected or leave our Old Adam in peace. To take the pastoral office upon yourself in Jesus' name means to open yourself to this power, both for forgiveness and for sanctification.

3. To take upon yourself the pastoral office in God's name also means, finally, to be ordained to disgrace and suffering for His name's sake. Christ is appointed for fall or rising. There is an important distinction, an uncomfortable rebuke, an opposition that never can be escaped where God works. An instrument in God's hand can never escape the

hard twisting and the harsh wear and tear against the world's ruggedness. There is a suffering that the Lord's servants really shall flee: that which is due to their own disobedience and their own neglect. The apostle says to see that "none of you suffer as a murderer or a thief or an evildoer or as a meddler. Yet if anyone suffers as a Christian, let him not be ashamed, but let him glorify God in that name" (1 Pet. 4:15–16 ESV). The suffering is not dangerous when it is suffering for the name of Jesus. When Paul was called to be an apostle, the Lord said, "Go, for he is a chosen instrument of mine to carry my name before the Gentiles and kings and the children of Israel. For I will show him how much he must suffer for the sake of my name" (Acts 9:15–16 ESV). To be willing to take upon yourself this office in His name means to be willing, as it says in Revelation, to bear much for His name's sake and seek to suffer as the apostles, who, when they were scourged and forbidden to speak in the name, went out from the council and rejoiced that there were counted worthy to be disgraced for His name's sake. It can mean to receive some of the same blessedness of which Peter talks: "if you are insulted for the name of Christ, you are blessed" (1 Pet. 4:14 ESV). Or to say with the Master's own words, "Blessed are you when people hate you and when they exclude you and revile you and spurn your name as evil, on account of the Son of Man! Rejoice in that day, and leap for joy, for behold, your reward is great in heaven; for so their fathers did to the prophets" (Luke 6:22–23 ESV).

In God's triune name, the pastoral office comes to be laid on you today who will thereby be our brothers in the office. All our inner desires of blessing, we gather together in that name. May all that you do in word or deed be done in His name. Then also in your office everything you do will give God glory and bless souls, yours and others. Let it be so. Amen.

Ordination Sermon for May 30, 1957

YOU ARE MY KING,
Psalm 44:3-4

for not by their own sword did they win the land,
nor did their own arm save them,
but your right hand and your arm,
and the light of your face,
for you delighted in them.
You are my King, O God;
ordain salvation for Jacob!

—Psalm 44:3–4 ESV

When this word speaks to us today at this ordination, it has three important things to say to us.

1. First it tells of the great kingdom of our fathers where God had carried out great things. "O God, we have heard with our ears, our fathers have told us, what deeds you performed in their days, in the days of old" (Ps. 44:1 ESV). It is great to be born in such a society, among people who know to speak of God, and to be able to grow up in a home where God's deeds in nature and church are a self-evident, secure, revered, and acknowledged basis for all of life. It is something of a calling and election to be able to grow up in a family or a home that speaks of the great deeds God carried out in the hearts of men through His Word. There is something that permeates the whole atmosphere of growing up that says what God said to His people through Moses: "Only take care, and keep your soul diligently, lest you forget the things that your eyes have seen, and lest they depart from your heart all the days of your life. Make them known to your children and your children's children" (Deut. 4:9 ESV). It is a great joy when God turns the hearts of children to their fathers, when they begin to speak with pride and thankfulness like the pious in Israel

about "the God of our fathers." God is always God. But for us men there is a comfort, a security, a joy that we have seen with our own eyes, what He has done among our fathers and with our ears has allowed us to hear what they could tell of their lives' rich experience. It is good to be able to say as King David, "In you our fathers trusted; they trusted, and you delivered them" (Ps. 22:4 ESV). And for a father's heart, there is hardly any greater joy on earth than to be able to experience the fulfillment of the promise in the Psalm: "In place of your fathers shall be your sons."

2. Next, this word tells us that the greatest inheritance from the fathers is this, that it impresses that the glory, the power, and all these valuable and great things of which we heard do not belong to our fathers, neither to any man. It all belongs to God alone. "For by their own sword they did not win the land, but your right hand and your arm, and the light of your face" (Ps. 44:3 ESV). Therefore the fathers point away from themselves; they point to Him who carries out the great deeds with His Word, He who with His right hand and His arm swings the Law's hammer and crushes hearts that are always as hard as stone, He who lets the light of His face shine from Christ's face and waken our faith in the promise of grace that an anxious heart always has such a hard time believing. So the fathers impress this, He has made us, and not we ourselves, into His people and into sheep in His herd. Therefore, neither can we say we are children of Abraham. We know that God alone brings up children to Him, creates the hearts of children from nature's hard hearts of stone. But it is this wonderful work, the Word's work of conversion and faith that we may see and hear about among the fathers. Because their love for us is double love, therefore they taught us seriously that the children of men are nothing and that he who has God does not need to ask for anything else in heaven or on earth. He who learns of them, he has learned to put all human work under the judgment of the Word. He has learned not to trust his own or any human work, but to trust faithfully and thankfully in the work that God carries out with His own arm, through His own Word, and he comes to pray again and again in the times when it goes well with him: "not to us, Lord, not to us, but to Your name be the glory."

3. But we still learn a third thing through this word. It is a teaching just for such lucky men who are spiritual heirs. It is a teaching that lies in the word "You the same are my King, O God."

You, the same, the same powerful God who carried out such powerful deeds in the time of the ancients, You are my King, O God. And now, of course, these great deeds do not depend on men. It was He who carried them out with His arm. His power is the same today. Who can set boundaries for His power? Who has the right to doubt and be discouraged when one has such a King? What have I to ask for with fear and trembling, if it is He who is my King? I must continually question myself and prove myself anew, if His mighty arm may work on my heart, if I myself stand under the Word's discipline, if I acknowledge my own faults, even when He changes the critique of men to detect them. But when His face shines on me, and I again have confidence that I am a child of Christ, and that He is my King and my Father, then I may also trust in my King's resources and my heavenly Father's power. Then I am not a spiritual heir of men, who poorly attempt to keep something of that by might that strong men carry out in spiritually richer times. The same God is my King. In His glory I am sent out. I have the same power to speak His Word. I am the Lord's servant and not man's. Going forward in my work does not depend on if I am successful compared to the work of others accomplishing what they did in their time. But it depends on if I am faithful to the Word, which alone can carry out the work. He who is my King, He leads His servants in all times, and He continually renews His work according to His own boundless council. It is when men are wholly and fully in His hand that one can completely and fully utilize the good inheritance He gave us through our fathers. Then one is not bound by the inheritance, but becomes richer. One does not feel as if he is standing under human compulsion, but under heavenly blessing. One no longer feels trapped and hemmed, but free to use all the blessed gifts that the Lord gave our fathers and us through them and use them rightly in God's time according to His direction in the freedom that is always where the Lord's spirit is. This then becomes a right faith in our rich inheritance. The Lord worked then, and the Lord will work now. The work shall be carried further, but it is the Lord's work. It depends on Him, and He alone determines it.

Therefore we will all today, those young in the work or those who have grown gray in it, dedicate ourselves anew to Him and His Word, thank Him for His work in times past, praise Him because His grace is constantly new, and with our hearts and mouths say,

> for not by their own sword did they win the land,
> nor did their own arm save them,
> but your right hand and your arm,
> and the light of your face,
> for you delighted in them.
> You are my King, O God;
> ordain salvation for Jacob! (Ps. 44:3–4 ESV)

Ordination Sermon for February 16, 1958

ALL SHALL BE FULFILLED,
Luke 18:31

And taking the twelve, he said to them, 'See, we are going up to Jerusalem, and everything that is written about the Son of Man by the prophets will be accomplished.'

—Luke 18:31 ESV

The Gospel lesson for the First Sunday in Lent is also a word for an ordination sermon. On the way to Jerusalem, it was a dark word that no one but the Master really understood, a word full of bad thoughts. For precisely that which was written through the prophets was a word about Him who was beaten for the sake of our misdeeds. But at the same time, it was a word full of deep mystery, a hidden light, for that which was written would in time cast light on the suffering and the cross and explain how all this could be a revelation of God's love. Once, on the road to Emmaus, Jesus would go through all the prophets and interpret them for the disciple—all that was written in the Scriptures was said about Him, the Messiah must suffer all this in order to enter His glory. Everything had happened according to God's good plans, and this plan God had included in the Word, the Word that must now be fulfilled.

At this time one was on the way up to Jerusalem, up against the climax of the drama, through which the world would be saved. Today we stand in the continuation of the same drama. That which happened in Jerusalem, also happened for our sakes. The drama on Golgotha would receive its continuation in Christ's Church. God's plans stretch further through time, up to the final culmination, where we are now on our journey, the day when Christ comes again and establishes His kingdom in power and glory. These plans are also found written in Scripture.

Jesus says of Himself before His ascension, "So it is written: the Messiah must suffer and on the third day He shall rise, and repentance and the forgiveness of sins shall be preached in His name to all people."

Even this word shall be fulfilled. We stand in the midst of this work today. For this reason we now have our ordination. All must be fulfilled that has been written about the Son of Man. The Gospel shall be preached to all people. We are called to see that it also happens in this diocese and at this time. Here is fulfilled a piece of God's plans, a piece of that which He determined from eternity and of which the Word witnesses. We have been able to be among them who would be His witnesses to the ends of the earth. A pastor is also on a journey with his Master to Jerusalem, up to the heavenly Jerusalem. And now all this that is written about the Son of Man shall be fulfilled.

It is written. For the pastor it is both a warning and a comfort to know that it is written that God revealed His intentions and wrote down His wisdom in the Word. It is this Word that the pastor has to proclaim. It shall be his passionate desire to be able to say with Paul, "For I did not shrink from declaring to you the whole counsel of God" (Acts 20:27 ESV). This is the Word he shall trust in all situations. The Scriptures, of course, cannot come to nothing, Jesus says. Not the smallest letter, not a jot or tittle, shall pass away before it has all been fulfilled. How should the Lord's called servants venture to change or cast away what their Lord has spoken?

It is also a comfort and security for the pastor to know that all shall be fulfilled. Here it is Christ who works, and the pastor is only put in line as a small link in this powerful event. Once, on the way up to Jerusalem, Jesus went alone, before the others who followed after trembling, as Mark tells us. So it has often been with the disciples. They do not understand. They don't know what will come. They are anxious about the future. But so He says to us again that all shall be fulfilled. We are small, small servants in a great work, soon forgotten and without possibility of keeping the threads together. But everything has its time just as it has been marked out. The forgiveness of sins shall be preached to all people. The seed shall fall out of the Son of Man's hand, and some falls on good earth. The nets are drawn through the sea and gather a catch of all different types of fish. The seed grows to size and does not know how. But one day the fruit is ripe, and then He lets the scythe go, for all that is written about the Son of Man must be fulfilled.

We all go into this work certain that our work cannot be in vain in the Lord. To the eyes of man, it can look as if we were distressed, irresolute, and beaten to the ground. But within all this, He goes on His way, and therefore nothing is hopeless and nothing is lost unless we lose Him. We will gladly give Him the promise that we are willing to drink of His cup and with Him go both to prison and in death. But we know how little our promise means. That which means all and that fills us with certainty is His promise. "See I am with you always, all shall be fulfilled that is written about the Son of Man."

Ordination Sermon for December 21, 1958

I SHALL GLADLY OFFER MYSELF,
2 Corinthians 12:15

I will most gladly spend and be spent for your souls. If I love you more, am I to be loved less?

—2 Corinthians 12:15 ESV

So also should a true pastor be able to say to his congregation. And there he has said something that is most noticeable for a true pastor. It is willingness to offer both himself and what is his for his congregation. It is not the willingness to die that makes him a true pastor. That can be found among those who fight for a godless despot or a false belief. But it is the true faith in Jesus Christ, the firm trust in the Word, and the honest desire to serve God with hand and mouth in the task he is given. Yet where this faith and this power is, there also comes a will to offer both himself and what is his. This will can also be found in other jobs and vocations. A pastor considers with reverence and thankfulness all the sacrifices that good men make for his own sake. Perhaps he remembers his mother or he thinks about his wife. He has seen doctors and politicians and many others sacrifice themselves to stressful work.

    Yet, there is still something particular about the pastor's work. If there is anything that gives us the right to speak of the holy pastoral office and the motivation, why it is delivered with such solemn ceremonies before God and with great account before the eyes, then it is what Paul says here: that the service, the work, and the sacrifice is for "your souls." Others apply to man's earthly, physical, and social best, that which Luther taught us to call the worldly kingdom. However, this is about God's spiritual kingdom, that which He does to save our souls and give us eternal life. After all, it does not help a person if she wins the whole world but has done damage to her soul, so the pastor's task is the most important of all because it concerns the soul and because the fruit belongs to eternity. Since this concerns the eternal well-being of men, negligence and laziness become doubly blameworthy. The pastor who understands what is at stake and why he is placed to preach to men, he can't but say, "I would gladly for your soul's sake sacrifice what I have and let myself spend and be spent."

One is consecrated for this sacrifice in a pastoral ordination. To be clothed with the pastoral office is to dedicate oneself to the Lord and His service, and His service is a service to the souls. Paul speaks about this priestly temple service that he carried out, and says that he was thereby "poured out as a drink offering upon the sacrificial offering of your faith." It is the love offering that a pastor can pour out with joy on the parish church altar. When he has been allowed to sow the Word, and it grows faith in the congregation, when the people come to the church and there one call follows the other to the Lord's Supper, then he can bend his knee to the altar and pour out the most precious of all offerings, the congregation's faith. Yet in this priestly service before God's face, he must be prepared to offer himself, just as Paul says in the same place where it says that his blood can now be poured out "over the sacrifice that I bring to God's altar, the sacrifice of your faith." At the time, he had martyrdom before his eyes. Many of our brothers in the pastoral office out in the world have it today. We have been spared "resisting till blood." But each pastor receives his measure of Christ's suffering for the sake of souls. Paul speaks therefore of the measure of Christ's suffering that his body must endure and that he carries out for Christ's Body that is the Church. So it is with each and every one who is ordained to Christ's service. There lies a measure of Christ's suffering and waiting. In our body we must endure them. That is to say, we must taste them and bear them in our body, our earthly existence, in the form of tiredness, disappointments, hard work, sleepless nights, mental pressure and bodily pain, sickness, and worries. And all shall be fulfilled for Christ's Body, that is, His Church, even for these men of flesh and blood that I am placed to lead to heaven. When my poor body suffers and is worn out in the service that has been my care, it happens for the benefit of the many other members in Christ's Body. Even this Paul has taught us: "If we are afflicted, it is for your comfort and your salvation." "So death is at work in us, but life in you."

It is a blessing to be able to be a pastor, to be able to bear the suffering that is destined to change to blessing and salvation. It is not as if this in any way should be compared to Christ's suffering that made propitiation and satisfaction. There is only one sacrifice that purifies from sin: the sacrifice of God's own Son. But we are placed to witness to that sacrifice. And if it means to bring forward that witness, then I shall gladly let myself be sacrificed, spend, and be spent. It is then that it can be granted for us to bear Jesus' wounds in our body, so that Jesus' life shall also be revealed in our body, in this our fragile earthly existence and our poor and defective deed.

Dear young brothers, you who now shall be our brothers in the office, today I want to wish you much of the joy that is in the pastor's vocation. But I will put ahead of all the wishes for you that which is perhaps the greatest joy: to also experience that suffering and toil, shame and agony can be a blessing from God, maybe even the richest and most fruitful in the pastor's life. May you sometime, when you can finally look back through the decades of pastoral service and your hair has grayed, think about all your labor and thankfully be able to say like Paul in his old age: "Therefore I endure everything for the sake of the elect, that they also may obtain the salvation that is in Christ Jesus with eternal glory" (2 Tim. 2:10 ESV).

Ordination Sermon for May 19, 1959

BE NOT DISMAYED, FOR I AM YOUR GOD,
Isaiah 41:10

> Fear not, for I am with you;
> be not dismayed, for I am your God;
> I will strengthen you, I will help you,
> I will uphold you with my righteous right hand.
> —Isaiah 41:10 ESV

So the Lord spoke to the Israel He had called and elected as His witness in the world. The same word and the same promise applies to everyone the Lord has elected to be his witness, even a Swedish priest in the twentieth century.

Fear not, be not dismayed, a person can have enough reason to both be afraid and be dismayed when considering the pastoral office. It would be ill of a priest to go out in his work sure of himself and conscious of his capacity. A priest always has reason to think: Who am I? How shall I, such a great sinner, be able to admonish others? A young priest has particular reason to ask himself: How shall I, with my slight experience, be able to be a teacher and a leader for others who have seen so much more of life than I? Look at me, I have often thought that it must look like ridiculous arrogance for me to dare step up and speak to all the great crowds of elders and professionals down before the pulpit.

But the Lord says, "Be not dismayed, for I am your God" (Isa. 41:10 ESV). Here lies the whole basis for a boldness and authority that is not boasting and arrogance. I am your God. God is God, the almighty and all-wise God. When He calls servants and witnesses, He does not command them to go out and witness from their own lives' rich experiences or to share of their own spirits' profundity. But He makes them heralds who take with them a message to proclaim. He makes them stewards and puts in their hands the Word and the Sacraments with which they are to work. He says, "I am your God. See, I put My Word in your mouth. Speak all that which I have commanded you. It is I, the Lord your God, who has said it. I will also watch over My Word." Here it is not about a wretched sinful little man that is more intelligent or experienced than others. But it is about a steward being faithful to his Lord, to herald the message without corruption. The right boldness comes from a humility that knows its own incompetence and inability, but that dares to trust in the power of God's Word.

Fear not, the Lord says. A pastor has many reasons to fear. It is not easy to be a pastor. The work is hard. The price we have to pay to be a servant of the Lord at this time is willingness to work without counting the work hours. We have too few pastors. A governmental report has shown that our priests on average have a much longer workday than is considered reasonable to otherwise expect of an employee. Human talk calls this an injustice. But we, who know what Lord we serve, ought not to complain but rather serve Him gladly. Worse than the long workday is the pressure that follows from again and again being ready at a particular time to step forward with a sterling and complete sermon. This can be particularly stressful for a young pastor. Right from the beginning, he is put under the same demands and must shoulder the same burdens as an experienced brother of the office. It is not surprising if he fears and wonders how he shall fare with it.

He may also have reason to fear when he thinks about the church's place in our land. A pastor is watched. If he makes a mistake it is noticed and possibly trumpeted in a manner that few other people run the risk of. The world likes to call itself tolerant, but there is one thing it rarely encounters with tolerance, and that is the living Church.

Yet the Lord says, "Fear not, for I am with you." The Savior never promised that it would be easy for His ambassadors, but He has promised to be with them always. It should never be routine work to proclaim God's Word, and the task doesn't get easier with time. The preacher never stands on his own legs. He is and will be dependent upon his Lord. If the Lord draws His hand back, then he must fail and fall. Yet He has promised to be with His servants, so long as the servant knows his dependence and supports himself on God. Again boldness rests completely upon this, that I do not trust myself, that I know that I cannot do this if I rely on myself, but that I also know what the Lord says: "I will strengthen you, I will help you." So surely has the Lord ordered it that His servants will always be dependent upon His help. So long as they know it and work accordingly, they need not fear opponents or enemies. Even the youngest of His servants can go out with that trust and hear the Lord's word to Jeremiah ringing in his ear: "But the Lord said to me, 'Do not say, "I am only a youth"; for to all to whom I send you, you shall go, and whatever I command you, you shall speak. Do not be afraid of them, for I am with you to deliver you, declares the LORD'" (Jer. 1:7–8 ESV).

And finally, the deepest reason for trust and joy in the Word: "I will uphold you with my righteous right hand" (Isa. 41:10 ESV). When a Christian hears these words, he thinks only about the righteousness of God that is revealed in Christ, God's righteousness for all those who believe and who are made righteous without corruption, by His grace through the propitiation in Christ Jesus. Here a true pastor has the rock to stand on that he knows never fails. The God who has given His own Son for us all, He does not tire of having mercy on His servants and forgiving them completely anew. And when He forgives anew, then it becomes certain again, certain both that He is there and that despite everything He will use me. Then I am willing again, willing to work without grumbling and without comparing my workday with others. I am bold again and glad to be able to serve such a Lord. And so I say again, to every one of you who now stands here to be consecrated into what is possibly the hardest and yet most glorious of all careers, I say it as a word from Him who called you to serve:

> fear not, for I am with you;
> be not dismayed, for I am your God;
> I will strengthen you, I will help you,
> I will uphold you with my righteous right hand. (Isa. 41:10 ESV)

Ordination Sermon for December 28, 1959

HIS FAITHFULNESS IS A SHIELD AND BUCKLER,
Psalm 91:4

His faithfulness is a shield and buckler.
—Psalm 91:4 ESV

So it is written about God in the Ninety-First Psalm, the great psalm about security under God's protection. It has something to say about the pastoral office too.

1. "His faithfulness is a shield and buckler." A pastor can say this when he steps into the office. When he asks how it came to be that he chose this way, the answer will always be that he didn't choose it himself. Behind his own decision stands another mightier will. Here cries a voice that says, "You have not chosen Me, but I have chosen you." How would someone dare choose such a path if it only meant to follow his own will? According to the human ways of seeing, there were completely different paths that seemed obvious, perhaps more attractive and rewarding. But God intervened and led me in a completely different way. He nudged me to take it. He broke down the obstacles even when they seemed insurmountable. When the pastor looks back, he has to say, "Truly it does not depend on my faithfulness that I became a pastor. But His faithfulness has been a shield and buckler. When I was tempted to give up or take another path, His faithfulness was there as a shield that blocked the other ways and nudged me and turned me so that I had to go the way He staked out."

2. "His faithfulness is a shield and buckler." A pastor can say this even more when he looks to the work of his office. There is much that

can bring fear and doubt. First of all, there is the uneasiness of not being sufficient, for not having something to give people from the pulpit in the long run and not being able to lead them right in soul care. If this depended on us and our own experience, we would do good first and foremost to give up our office. But now we have a resource that means more than everything else: His faithfulness. He who has given the task is responsible for the power and the resources that we need. He gives us His Word with an inexhaustible treasure of wisdom and experience. He bids us to use up these riches, to take for ourselves what we need and to distribute it to others. Here is the answer to all the questions that will meet us in the future. Here is the substance of our sermons and the wisdom we need as *seelsorger*s. And in His faithfulness He will make this Word to be our shield and buckler. When His servants keep the Word and live by it, the faithful God, in every new setting and in every new difficulty, holds up this shield to protect us and lead us on the certain path. So we dare in the power of His faithfulness to boldly take hold of it, as we never would have been able to of our own accord.

3. "His faithfulness is a shield and buckler." This applies even more in the strife and before all the opposition that a true pastor must meet. Because Christ is a sign that will be spoken against, so the servant of Christ will be spoken against. There is a share of Christ's Gospel that people will not hear. It can be the demand for courage to say all that the Lord has commanded. It can mean that one must risk his reputation and popularity. The temptation can come and show that it is best to pass it by or be silent. He says that it is only a question of interpretation concerning God's Word. After all, there is always someone who interprets it otherwise and reads something into it other than what is really there. Before all temptations to say something other than God's Word says, we may only answer, "His faithfulness is a shield and buckler. I am safe under His shield. It is His Word and not mine, His thing and not mine. I will be faithful, simple and unsophisticatedly faithful to the message He gives me to deliver, since I know that I can leave everything else to Him."

4. "His faithfulness is a shield and buckler." It is in the end also my comfort and security when I stand there as an unfaithful steward, a lazy servant who again needs to confess his great sin. His faithful mercy seems only to become greater with the years. He not only has patience with His servants, He knows also to use their mistakes to strengthen them and often He uses their mistakes as a blessing. It is as it is written in the Psalms: He instructs sinners on the way. He leads the humble rightly. He leads sinners in the right way for His name's sake. Yes, all the Lord's

ways are grace and faithfulness for those who keep His covenant and testimony.

And you, to whom we may now say, "Dear brothers of the office," you who desire to take the holy pastoral office that is entrusted to you today, we desire that it would mean for each and every one you an ever-deeper experience of God's faithfulness. This happens when you go the way that you know so well, the sinner's way to the Savior in daily repentance, in repentance and faith. It is the only way that leads to God, even for a pastor. It is a path full of humility, but even more blessing even for a pastor. Faithful is He who calls you; He shall also complete His work. Amen.

Ordination Sermon May 30, 1960

ON CHRIST'S BEHALF,
2 Corinthians 5:20

Therefore, we are ambassadors for Christ.
—2 Corinthians 5:20 ESV

This is the significance of the pastoral office as Paul once expressed it with classical clarity. On Christ's behalf, it means this: in His place, by His command, to represent Christ, to carry out His errands. We are ambassadors; this means we come with a message from Him, sent as ambassadors to put forward His demands and bring forward His offer. We know that as long as we carry out His command, He Himself stands behind the order with all His power. Then, he who hears us hears Christ. It is God who makes His appeal through us. He who rejects us, he rejects Christ himself. For on Christ's behalf we are ambassadors.

An ambassador, it also means one who is sent out. He has received a command to go out. His Lord has said, "Go out. See, I send you. You shall be My witness." The savior sends each and every one who is assigned his task as His ambassadors to be witnesses in Jerusalem and all of Judea and Samaria and then to the ends of the world. So He also gives His ambassadors to each and every one of His congregations. And where I have been placed, there I know that I have His command to be an ambassador on His behalf. I do not need to ask if I am welcome, if men wish to hear this message. I come on behalf of Him who has created all these people, who has redeemed them and given His blood for them. We pray on Christ's behalf; be reconciled with God.

He who has received such an order no longer belongs to himself. From that hour when I was ordained to be a pastor and became my Lord's ambassador, I am also Christ's serf. "Woe to me, if I do not proclaim the gospel," Paul says. Our Fathers used to cite the prophet: "Cursed is he who does the work of the LORD with slackness" (Jer. 48:10 ESV). This ordination applies a lifelong service. It applies to all of my life and my being. "He yearns jealously over the spirit that he has made to dwell in us" (James 4:5 ESV). It is bad if a Christian is either cold or warm. It is doubly bad if Christ's ambassadors, who are supposed to speak and act on His behalf, attempt the impossible and try to love both God and the world. Therefore James also says this strict word to the teachers of the congregation: "You know that we who teach will be judged with greater strictness" (3:1 ESV).

But he who is an ambassador on Christ's behalf ought also to know that all the grace that he is sent to proclaim to others also applies to him. When he admonishes on Christ's behalf, "be reconciled with God," so he himself has the right to be the first to trust the admonishment. He may drink again and again from the cup of salvation. He may follow Paul and as the first among sinners hold fast to this, that it is a firm word worth receiving, that Christ Jesus comes to the world to save just such sinners.

One such ambassador of Christ, who lives by the Lord's mercy and who at the same time will serve Him uprightly, may also trust that the Lord does not forget those He sends out into the world. He said Himself, "See, I am with you always." He has promised that His Spirit shall dwell in us and live in us. He has told us that we are worth more than many sparrows, of which not one falls to the ground apart from God's will. Already here on earth He prayed for them who through our word, our preaching, would come to faith in Him. We can be certain that this prayer also continues in His heavenly intercession, when He exhorts good for us. In this prayer nothing is forgotten. All the great work, in all its small, small details are included. Every little ambassador, even those in what seems the most forsaken outpost, even in the most difficult conditions, is yet an ambassador on behalf of Christ, and his Lord is with all that He has laid on him to do—in every sermon, at every Baptism and Lord's Supper, every hospital visit, every conversation concerning the care of the soul, every confirmation lesson, every children's sermon.

To this great work, to be Christ's ambassadors, you are ordained today, you who now stand here before God's altar, when Christ today entrusts you with salvation's Word and makes you stewards of His Sacrament, so occurs the greatest and best intervention that can happen with a man. May this be a living reality for your hearts. May you be able to say as the prophet: "O LORD, you have deceived me, and I was deceived; you are stronger than I, and you have prevailed" (Jer. 20:7

ESV). May it go for you as with the prophet so that on the day when God's Word makes you "a laughingstock all the day," whom "everyone mocks," so you too will not be able to quit speaking because of the fire in your heart, and therein is contained a fire against which no one can fight and no one can extinguish. There is a fire that the Lord tends in an upright heart, in a weak and sinful man, when He says to you, "from this day shall you be My ambassador, it is I who appeal through you, fear not, for I am with you." Amen.

Ordination Sermon for December 20, 1960

THE GOSPEL, THE POWER OF GOD,
Romans 1:16

*For I am not ashamed of the gospel,
for it is the power of God for salvation.*
—Romans 1:16 ESV

It has been hard to confess Christ and easy to be ashamed of the Gospel in every age. So it is in our age too, even for a pastor.

Why is it so easy to be ashamed of the Gospel? Naturally, because the Gospel is not something that we men can conceive of by our natural reason. It lies outside of all our daily experience. No one has to be ashamed of a common, speculative belief in God. It is accepted by reason, if for nothing else, as an interesting discussion starter. Neither does one have to be ashamed of a moralistic idealism. It is in line with what the conscience and the concept of justice say about every man. But that God would give His only Son so that everyone who believes in Him should not perish, that has always been an obstacle and stumbling block. It is something that we have not been able to imagine. That God administers justice and does not tolerate anything, that is logical. But that He Himself dies in order to atone for our misdeeds, that is not something that we could have thought probable. And that even a moral person's small everyday sins can be so severe so as to separate her so completely from God, that even she must be saved through such a sacrifice, that is most challenging to ethical idealism that will reason for itself and hold to its own capabilities.

Therefore the Word of salvation has a strange and repulsive clang to the ears of the world. To need salvation to be saved, to have a savior, they all become something before which one feels a little embarrassed or maybe superior. So it was in Paul's time, and so it is in our day. But all the more certainly Paul says, "I am not ashamed of the gospel."

This is something every pastor in our day can learn to say, to train himself to say, pray for grace to be able to say, firmly and confidently, as an inner certainty, so that as the years go by it becomes so controlling that he doesn't need to say it or think it because it constantly fills his being and speaks out of his disposition and deeds.

How does one receive such a confident boldness?

First and foremost by constantly keeping clear whose work he is doing. We are sent out by Christ, on His behalf. We are His ambassadors. It is God who makes His appeal through us, Paul says. What we say is not our own philosophy, not speculation that we learned from others and found to be probable, not a summary of that which we have found to be best of the world's wisdom and poetry. But we speak what Christ commands His ambassadors to speak. With this message He commanded them to go out and make disciples of all people. We continue the work in their wake. The same exhortation that the apostle once gave his nearest successor applies to us: "hold fast to what you have learned. Guard the good deposit entrusted to you with the help of the Holy Spirit. Keep a close watch on yourself and your teaching, for by this you will save both yourself and those who hear you."

For the Gospel is the power of God for salvation. It is for this reason that God has sent it out into the world. For this reason He has hidden His power in it, the power that makes Christ, the Risen One, living even for us, so that His work happens even in our day and saves us too. Nothing other than the Gospel can do this. For nothing else has God's power.

For this reason a pastor must not be ashamed of the Gospel. It shall be his joy to preach it. He shall not duck in embarrassment when one expects notification of life and death, of salvation and perdition. He shall not try to strengthen his right to existence or try to make the Church more acceptable by preaching good morals or good psychology that can help a person adapt to society or overcome his feelings of isolation. Here the word applies, "seek first after God's kingdom and His righteousness, and everything else will be given to you." "What does a man gain if he wins the whole world but loses his soul?" Therefore, a pastor shall preach Christ, preach Law and Gospel to repentance and faith.

This is true boldness that is not ashamed of the Gospel, but this demands that the pastor lives by the Gospel, that it is and remains God's power and salvation for himself. Here again it is a question of faithfulness in the calling, of being faithful in his own study of the Bible and his own devotions, of the humility and repentance when Christ's Word strikes at our own failings, about willingness to bow himself before the Spirit's chastisement and ask both God and man for forgiveness, and of constantly holding to Christ, trusting in Christ and living before Christ's face.

Pastors can be so different. The gifts are so different, through God's good direction. But in one thing all true and faithful pastors are the same, both those gifted in the theoretical and those gifted in the practical, both the shy and the personable, both the famous and those who live unnoticed, they are all Christ's servants, they love their Lord, they trust in Him. He is their only Savior without whom they could not think to live even one day.

May God unite you all who stand here to be such pastors, Christ's pastors who cannot live without Him even for one day. Amen, Amen.

Ordination Sermon for March 6, 1961

I HAVE CALLED YOU BY NAME,
Isaiah 43:1

> *But now thus says the Lord,*
> *he who created you, O Jacob,*
> *he who formed you, O Israel:*
> *Fear not, for I have redeemed you;*
> *I have called you by name, you are mine.*
>
> —Isaiah 43:1 ESV

This is the Lord's word to His people Israel, those whom He had called and given a mission among all other people: "You are My witness, and I am your God."

So can God speak to every baptized person. He has called us by name and said, "You are mine." Already in the moment when we received our own name, we received it under His hands of blessing. We received a mission in the world, a calling, a purpose in life, a hope for eternity. Again God says: "You are My witness, and I am God."

God can say this in a particular way to him who would become a pastor: "I have called you by your name, you are Mine." He has heard this call in his heart. It was he who received from Him the resolve to become a pastor. The resolve can be hard. The way can be long. And still, where there is this call, it does not miss us. He says again and again, "I have called you by name. You are Mine. You shall be My witness, and I am God."

And when a man receives wisdom and boldness to follow the call, it is this that becomes a secure foundation for all my life and all my work. The Lord has said, "You are Mine."

It is a help in temptation and a powerful invitation to daily repentance. If God has said that I am His, and I have stayed at my post, where

I shall do His work and be His messenger, then I may not be ashamed of His name. If He has given me this undeserved confidence, then I must give Him my strength, all my zeal, all my faith and trust. If He has made me His, then I will also be His with all my heart and being.

But it is also a powerful comfort, something that helps and carries me. It is God who has called me. He has called me with the heart's calling and led me on paths that I myself could not see. But He has also crafted His call with visible signs. In order that it should not be just my own undertaking, not just something that I have built upon my own feeling of being called, God has given His Church the mission to call servants on His behalf, to test them and ordain them. I may also receive the call in God's house, before His altar, delivered by this congregation of God's through the tools God has determined. Even here, I am called by name, and God says again, "You are Mine, My witness, My servant, My own."

"You are My witness. Fear not, but speak all that I ask you." This is the great comfort before the hard task of preaching God's Word. It is not just something that comes from me. I have received it from God, as a talent, a mission, a greeting from Him to men, a sound teaching. Therefore I always have a way out and a help in my incompetence. I can sit down and read and learn, listen and ponder. I know that I have my God and my Savior in His Word. When He says, "You are Mine," then I know that He promises to lead me with His Word, to give me clarity and wisdom, when I deepen my understanding in His Word.

"You are Mine." This also means that I may believe that He comes to put His hand on me even with all my sin. He has given me this hard service with all these responsibilities, so He will also give me His help with all the mercy and grace that is His. Therefore I will reply, quietly and thankfully, day after day, in all toils and difficulties, "Yes, You are my God, and I am Yours."

Ordination Sermon for May 19, 1961

THE MESSENGER IS NOT GREATER THAN HE WHO SENT HIM,
John 13:16

Truly, truly, I say to you, a servant is not greater than his master, nor is a messenger greater than the one who sent him.
—John 13:16 ESV

Jesus tells this to His apostles. It may well seem a self-evident thing. Still He found it necessary to remind them of this, that they, as His servants, were not greater than their Lord, and as His messengers were not greater than He who was to give them their mission.

Even today the Lord Jesus Christ sends servants and messengers to follow in the footsteps of the apostles, to continue the work to which He sent them out. Even today Christ's messengers need this reminder: "Truly, truly, I say to you, a servant is not greater than his master, nor is a messenger greater than the one who sent him" (John 13:16 ESV).

A pastor is a messenger (an ambassador) on the Lord's errand. He has full authority to speak in his Lord's name. He comes with a greeting from God Himself. Therefore Jesus says, "Whoever receives the one I send receives me, and whoever receives me receives the one who sent me" (John 13:20 ESV). Therefore, one's eternal destiny is decided by the message that the pastor carries. So he can forgive anyone his sins or bind him to them in Jesus' name. Therefore, Paul also says that it is God who makes His appeal through us. He says that it is the Holy Spirit who has placed us as stewards to be shepherds for God's congregation.

For this very reason, the Lord Christ now gives us this reminder, that the messenger is not greater than the one who sent him.

It was when He had washed His disciples' feet that He uttered these words: "If I then, your Lord and Teacher, have washed your feet, you also ought to wash one another's feet" (John 13:14 ESV). He who was their Lord, and the whole world's Lord, had done a service that was the least among services. So through this deed he had shown what He means when He said, "The greatest among you shall be your servant." Jesus Himself says that this is contrary to the world's order. There, those who would be princes of the people appear as lords, and let others know their authority, but it is not so in His kingdom. He made Himself destitute; He who is all-powerful came to us in the form of a servant. And he who will be Christ's servant, he may not be greater than his Lord.

It also means that there is no place to serve that is capable of being beneath the pastor's worthiness. After all, the Church lives in this world and has its own outer civil order, so it becomes easy for the world to grade men also in the Church's service. In many contexts a pastor might receive an esteemed place, if he is not at the top. In all this he shall know in his heart that he is sent by Him who came as a servant even though He was Lord of lords. And he shall always be ready to show it. It is true that he is set to preach the Gospel, to administer the Sacraments, to guard souls, and lead the congregation. He shall not entertain any other possibilities. And then he may have constant occasion to take seriously that the Lord's steward is everyone's slave. Ever and again he will have occasion to show it in his pastoral work. He may sacrifice his own comfortableness, always be prepared to be disturbed, stay in service when no one else would do it and in quiet and unremarkable work when others are enjoying their free time, or sleep which is obviously right. God constantly gives him new occasions to do small or great services for men that have nothing to do with his office, but which still show that he stands in service to his Lord who washed His disciples' feet.

But all this means only one thing, that the messenger is not greater than the one who sent him. Jesus said it Himself when He sent out the seventy-two: "It is enough for the disciple to be like his teacher, and the servant like his master. If they have called the master of the house Beelzebul, how much more will they malign those of his household" (Matt. 10:25 ESV).

Even on this point it is easy for the pastor to begin thinking the thoughts of men. We have been so accustomed to living in a land that is at least Christian in name that many Christians don't take it seriously that being a Christian will mean persecution, slander, and defamation. And it shows itself in every generation anew, suffering for Christ shall not end. It shows itself most where men in obedience to the Lord Christ begin to live in a manner different than their surroundings. All this ought to be most clear for pastors. It may be enough for him if it goes for him as it did for his Master. He is, of course, not greater than his Lord. On the contrary, he is called and ordained to share His shame and bear his measure of suffering for Christ. When they come, he shall greet them as a sign of his Lord's faithfulness. He shall not be resentful or be bitter, but say to himself that the messenger cannot be greater than the Lord, who is the one who sent him. It also belongs to our mission to share His suffering to be like Him by bearing His wounds and letting His abusers' abuse fall on us.

Today you celebrate, you who stand here before the Lord's altar, ordained as Christ's ambassadors and as His servants. During all your labor and difficulties, you can commit this to memory, that you are ambassadors on behalf of Christ. It is enough for you if it goes for you as for your Lord. If Christ's suffering comes on us, the apostle says, then through Christ comfort will come for us too in overflowing measure. He who lives by His forgiveness and constantly anew receives it, he also receives everything else he needs. May all that meets you carry you deeper in communion with Him, in suffering and joy, to destruction for that which shall die, and to resurrection and new life, glory to Him, and blessing to you and many, many others. Amen.

Ordination Sermon for December 28, 1961

WE HAVE RECEIVED THIS MINISTRY BY THE MERCY OF GOD,
2 Corinthians 4:1

Therefore, having this ministry by the mercy of God, we do not lose heart.
—2 Corinthians 4:1 ESV

"This ministry" ("this office") is the same that will be delivered to you who stand here before the altar, that which in our pastoral ordination rite is called the holy pastoral office.

It is an office, a mission that comes from God, a call that one is ordained to for the rest of his life.

The mission that comes from God is the mission that witnesses of His grace, the Gospel, to be ambassadors on Christ's behalf, to bring forward God's Word so that God Himself makes His appeal through us. The office is therefore called the office of reconciliation. God who was in Christ and reconciled the world to Himself has entrusted us with the Word of reconciliation. This Word is important for the blessing of men. Where it shines, men can be reconciled with God. There sins can be forgiven, however great they may be. There men can be children of God, no matter how frail their character or their capacity to do the good that they would and leave alone the evil they would not do. For this Word and these Sacraments give pure forgiveness, and there where it is received in faith all is forgiven. And so that this would happen, God has instituted the office of reconciliation, the pastoral office. And it is of this office of reconciliation that Paul now says we have this office.

Therefore Paul also says that he regards his office highly. He knows that he has received it from God. He knows that God has given this mission to him. It defines his whole life. He is not just a Christian like all the others. He has this particular mission, this office. And a pastor should know this. The world already knows it. It knows, yet perhaps with a certain loathing. Maybe it ridicules the office. It looks at the pastor as someone notable and strange, before whom one feels a little unsure or artificial. The pastor will take all this with great composure. He shall not attempt to convince men that he is "just a normal man." He is not. He has this office.

But if the pastor has this mission from God, then he has every reason to regard it highly, but this does not mean that he himself is something higher or more notable than a normal sinner. Paul also reminds us of this matter, in this word. He says that we have this ministry "which we received by the mercy of God." It is not for the sake of our merits that we have received it. It is God's mercy. It is already on account of God's mercy that we are Christians, that we were born in a Christian land and were baptized. It is God's mercy that we live in the forgiveness of sins that we need every day. And it is God's mercy that we are called and ordained into this office. We have deserved none of this. We can earn none of it. In our account with God, we are always in the red. We have not loved Him above all things one single day of our lives. It is really, literally His grace that He is not finished with us, that He has not long ago stopped forgiving and sent us away for good. A pastor can often wonder how it came to be that God called him to this great mission. And he can only say the same as Paul, that he is one because the Lord's mercy is overflowing, because mercy is applied to the steward, and because mercy is constantly new, he may remain in the ministry. What he cannot do is neglect the mercy, cease to seek it, finish testing himself, quit confessing his sins, and quit coming to his Lord Christ empty-handed to live by His mercy. He who has this office can never have it in the right manner, if he does not live by his Lord's mercy. He cannot handle the office of reconciliation if he does not himself live in the mystery of reconciliation.

But *for this reason*, Paul now says, "Therefore, having this ministry by the mercy of God, we do not lose heart" (2 Cor. 4:1 ESV).

If we didn't have this ministry, this office, then there would be no foundation for our boldness. Had we not had this mission from God, but were only placed in it by men, were we not ordained by God to this, but had only been led to this mission by our own inner feelings or desire or sensation, how would we then dare to stand there when one's own inclination ended or when men refuse to hear and listen? Were this only a work commanded because men have a religious need every once in a while, then it would not be easy to keep heart in the headwind and difficulties, and just as ill would it be if the mission depended on our worthiness and not on mercy. What would we then do, when God's own good Word holds us accountable for negligence, misunderstanding, and tired and failing disciples?

But now we have this office. We have received it from God, and we have received it by God's mercy. We have received it for the sake of men because they need the Gospel. And they need it whether we are more or less successful. The Word, the message, is just as true and important whether we know joy and success or not. So, we do not lose heart. What happens here is what God has commanded. It is my calling in life to preach this Gospel and administer these Sacraments. It happened according to the Lord's command and by His conviction. I need not make myself anxious about how it will end. I shall sow and sow, preach and instruct, appeal and comfort, absolve, baptize, and celebrate the Lord's Supper. I have this office.

We who have had this office for a long time, we could possibly say something about how over the years it became clearer and easier to know that we have it completely and thoroughly by God's mercy, that every new day of work is a gift of His mercy, who does not tire of forgiving His decrepit servants. And we will wish you who today receive this office that this will all the more be a sense of certainty and joy in work, that you know and understand that it is God who has done this, that it is He who gave the mission, and that it rests completely and thoroughly on His mercy.

Ordination Sermon for May 29, 1962

GIVE ME YOUR HEART,
Proverbs 23:26

My son, give me your heart, and let your eyes observe my ways.
—Proverbs 23:26 ESV

He is a good father, one of the wise men of Israel who says this. He speaks on God's behalf, for it is God's statutes and laws to which he will gain his son. And he knows that it depends on the son embracing these with his heart. For if the heart is far away, then what the lips tell the hands to do does not help.

Therefore God could Himself say this to each and every one of us: "My son, give me your heart" (Prov. 23:26 ESV). There is a lot more that God expects of His pastors. He seeks faithfulness from us, first and foremost faithfulness to His Word, so that we really will carry His own Word and dare to speak what He asks us. He expects that we will pay attention to His teaching, take great pains to find the right meaning in God's Word, and watch our instruction. God expects many other good and important things of His servants too: that we should be willing to suffer, that we should not be sluggish in our zeal, that we should not be looking out for our own benefit. But that is why this call is so infinitely important: "My son, give me your heart."

It is something that isn't very visible. It cannot be written in any church law nor proven by any exam. It cannot be controlled by any superior. It is a hidden matter, a matter between the pastor and his God, but yet so important.

My son, give Me your heart. Life proceeds from the heart. If God has my heart, then He has all of me. Then there is nothing left that I can keep for myself. With the heart I shall believe. With the heart's desire, I shall embrace my Savior; the Word will be kept in pure and good hearts. God will make of us obedient hearts. The Word says all this. And it reminds us of the same when the Savior asks His piercing question: Simon, son of John, do you love Me? Do you love Me?

Do I love You, Lord?

Why do I do all this? What is it that drives me to serve my Lord? Perhaps first and foremost this: that I am honestly convinced that He is true, that He really has come from God and revealed the Father to us. More than that, that I know what His Gospel and His Church have given man. Perhaps, I have seen how poor life is without Him. I have seen how forlorn men are and distressed when they attempt to live without Him. In Him and His Church my life has found meaning. It has received splendor and depth. And yet, it is not enough. "Simon, son of John, do you love Me?"

The question stands there at the beginning of our ministry, on our ordination day. It follows a pastor through the years. During which it may be a word of reproach that goes right through the heart: "I know you are enduring patiently and bearing up for my name's sake, and you have not grown weary. But I have this against you, that you have abandoned the love you had at first" (Rev. 2:3-4 ESV).

How can I be certain that I have given the Lord my heart? The more I test my heart, the more I try to force it to love completely and thoroughly, the better I understand why the Scriptures say, "The heart is deceitful above all things, and desperately sick; who can understand it?" (Jer. 17:9 ESV). And if I once believed that salvation would lie in this, that I gave God my heart completely and unsparingly, so I understand all the more how impossible it is for me to do it with such a heart, and I am ashamed to come with such a gift to God.

And then He says: "My son, give me your heart."

And the apostle says that if our hearts condemn us, then God is greater than our heart. His fatherly heart loves His children with an eternal love. He makes it possible that even our evil and impure heart would be able to desire to be with Him and be His. For this it needs a Mediator, a suffering Savior, a Righteous One who leads the unrighteous. "In this is love, not that we have loved God, but that he loved us and sent his Son to be the propitiation for our sins" (1 John 4:10 ESV). It also means this: this is salvation, not that we can give God a pure heart, but that God has given us His Son and with Him gave us sinners righteousness, so that we now can say, "Abba, Father."

"My son, give me your heart." So the Father says, He who gave us sinners righteousness. He does not desire here what no one can give: a pure heart and a devotion that never falters, but He desires faith that grasps His promise. He puts forward His Son and asks us to come to Him and believe in Him. And here we may answer, "Lord, to whom shall we go? You have the words of eternal life. You are the Messiah, the Son of the living God. Lord it is good that we are here; Lord stay here with us."

And then He has our heart, and we are His brothers and coheirs, and His Father is our Father, then God has also received the hearts of His children, just as He will have them.

Now, this is the most important of all for a pastor too, for just this reason we are reminded of this in this hour.

So, I come, my God, to find true joy in Jesus' name, In firm faith to say, my Father, I am Your child, knowing that You hear my prayer, amidst a life of trial, Your promise, Your Word, done faithfully to Your fame. Amen.

Ordination Sermon for December 30, 1962

WE LIVE WITH HIM BY HIS POWER,
2 Corinthians 13:4

For he was crucified in weakness, but lives by the power of God. For we also are weak in him, but in dealing with you we will live with him by the power of God.
—2 Corinthians 13:4 ESV

This word is written by Paul in a disturbed moment in a letter that is stamped more than any other with the suffering and strain of standing as a shepherd and apostle among insubordinate, skeptical, and complacent parishioners, full of all types of wretches and all types of human opinions. The letter is the second to the Corinthians. We notice how it hurts Paul that everything he does, says, and writes is distorted and misinterpreted by his critics. He had worked long into the nights with his tent-making business so as not to be a burden to anyone. Now one hears that he is weak and does not demand respect. He has written seriously and pleadingly. Now he hears that it is not something to worry about that he can be strict and authoritative enough in his letter, "but in person he is weak and what he says makes no impression." What he says makes no impression. One notices the superiority, "what he says . . ."; one sweeps it under as if it were only Paul who spoke. And then Cajus and Crispus, Sextus and Publius just as well come with their special opinions. And yet Paul knows that he is an ambassador on behalf of Christ, that it is God who makes His appeal through him, and that he who rejects him rejects Christ. Still anyone can speak against this word. It has no visible power. The apostle must find that it is so. Among the Corinthians he really appeared "in great weakness." He says it himself.

And when he is now treated contemptuously for the sake of his great weakness, he answers by pointing to his Lord Christ. There was weakness in Him too, and power. He became, Paul says, crucified in weakness. Helpless in appearance, He was given up to His executioners. His opponents went and spit on Him. They scornfully showed that He did not help Himself—He did not come down from the cross. Neither did God come to His help. Even concerning Him, they self-assuredly would say, "In person He is weak, and when He appears He doesn't make an impression." Yet Paul says that even if He was crucified in weakness, so He lives by the power of God. He lives. This was God's way: first frustration, shame and the cross, and then the resurrection glory and all authority in heaven and on earth. It was God's way that Jesus laid out for His disciples on the way to Emmaus: the Messiah must suffer all this before entering His glory. His kingdom is really not of this world, where one forces his own will with power and makes his enemies bow under him like a dictator. He did not come to condemn the world but to save it, not to beat down the evil and contentious and disobedient but to suffer in their place and bring redemption for their disobedience. And His Gospel is the Word of redemption. The pastoral office is the office of redemption. It means that the Gospel, the Church, and the pastor live here in the world and step before men in the same weakness and frustration as with Christ Himself, the suffering and crucified. Even we are weak in Him, says Paul. He has received the experience a hundred times "during persecution's distress and suffering, during the blows, the toil, the vigils and famine," during "danger from compatriots, danger from heathen, danger among false brothers." This is what his false brothers have discovered and scorned him for. He is weak. But he is weak in Christ. It is Christ's suffering he suffers, the same suffering as Christ and His Gospel must suffer, because they hide their power and come with the Word of reconciliation.

But here comes the other side of the matter. Paul does not forget it. It is this that carries him. God's power that raised our Lord Christ from the dead, it lives also in His Gospel and in His Church. We have been baptized not only into His death but also into His resurrection, not only into His suffering but also into His victory and glory. We live by this power. Even though it is hidden, it still works in us, it carries us, and it makes it so that we never need to lose heart. And when He is revealed, it will be revealed with Him in His overwhelming glory.

To this weakness and to this power a pastor is ordained when he is ordained as Christ's servant and messenger in the holy pastoral office. He is ordained to share in Christ's weakness. On Christ's behalf, he shall appeal to men to be reconciled to God, knowing well that anyone can reject the appeal, perhaps with scorn and blasphemy. Others come to understand that they understand the matter better and do not need any guide. Others come to listen and receive and are called to the Church, but in their lives they start showing profound trust in the Gospel's transforming power. And during all this, the pastor will not be sore, not be violent, not be disappointed and lose heart, but will be calm and will inwardly continue to exhort and pray, invite and instruct, just like his Lord commanded him. Many times, he comes to wish that he should put authority behind his word. But he continually comes to hear his Lord's voice anew; for the disciple it is enough if it goes for him as with his Master. "If they have rejected Me, so shall they reject you."

But at the same time the pastor is ordained to be part of this same power of Christ, there is strength in weakness. He comes to see that this scoffed-at and authority-lacking Gospel cannot be conquered; even when we are pressed from all sides, we are never without a way out. We can be beaten to the ground but never lost. In the midst of all this, we win a glorious victory. We live by God's power with him. And so Paul adds, that you should know. He says it to his Corinthians for whom he cares so much, who caused him so much worry, and where so many openly showed contempt for him. From him, the weak one, they still come to know that God's power lives in his weakness.

A pastor may remember this too. He shall refrain from the power that fights for its right and its glory, its place and its prestige among men. However in this weakness shall Christ live with His power and manifest itself in the congregation among men. The *how* cannot be known in advance. Here, a person can only believe without seeing. The promise is there. Just when I am weak, I am strong. Just there in the earthen vessel is the treasure. God's weakness is stronger than men. And He is able to do more, yes much more than that for which we pray or think, according to the power that is really in us. To Him belongs the glory in the congregation and in Christ Jesus and all generations forever and ever. Amen.

Ordination Sermon for May 20, 1963

YOU ARE MY WITNESSES,
Isaiah 43:12

> I declared and saved and proclaimed,
> when there was no strange god among you;
> and you are my witnesses," declares the Lord, "and I am God.
> —Isaiah 43:12 ESV

"You are my witnesses." It is God who says this. Does God need witnesses? Can one be a witness for God?

It is certain; no one would dare to be God's witness if he understood what this means—"I am God"—that is, provided God has not commanded it. But when He commands, then one must obey. Then one must go out and witness, precisely because he is God.

To be a pastor is to be God's witness. To be a true pastor, it means knowing that one is God's witness, wanting to be God's witness, not wanting to be anything but a witness for God.

The pastor should know that he is God's witness. What should he witness to? God says it in the same place by the prophet. "I, I am the LORD, and besides me there is no savior. I declared and saved and proclaimed" (Isa. 43:11–12 ESV). There is something that God has proclaimed and announced. There is something God has done: He has gained salvation. God has also spoken and done. And now He gives messengers to witness to this. The messenger has nothing to come with that he himself has thought of or figured out. He is a witness. Just as a witness before court may not add anything either because he wishes it were so or because someone else hopes that he will say it, so the pastor shall not touch upon any of that which he himself or others think but witness to that which God has announced and that which

God has done. He doesn't interpret his own thoughts or feelings. He is a witness.

How can one be a witness to that which happened so long ago? It is because God, when He had said and done this had every future era in His thoughts. It was said and done so that it would be proclaimed here on earth as long as there were people. Therefore God included all that He had said and done to gain our salvation in His Word, in a message that He formed according to His will and that He sent out so that it should also reach us. God now works in this Word. He works on man's heart. He enters into conversation with us. Here, Christ is always among us. Here the same happens that happens when a man learns to know a woman and becomes certain about who the woman is, what she does, what she means and wants and plans. So God, the triune, enters into conversation with us and makes Himself known as a living experience so real and so near that one can say, "You are my God. My eyes have seen Your salvation."

Therefore, that a pastor will want to be God's witness and nothing other than God's witness means two things. First, he will not speak or do anything other than that which his Lord has commanded him. He will not witness about himself or about some other human thoughts that speak to him. He will instead carefully find out what it is God wants him to witness to, what He has said and done. Therefore he loves this Word and deepens his knowledge of it. He learns to know it better with every new year that he remains in his Lord's service.

But it also means that he will be a real witness who has himself been able to see and be part of this that God speaks about here. It means that he receives the Word first and foremost in his own heart. When the Word punishes and hurts, and it does that at times, he does not waver under it, but he stands under the discipline and endures it. At first this may touch upon his own comfort and irritability, his own half-truths and unkindness, his own desire for fame or to be left alone. But just for this reason the Gospel, the promise, the comfort applies to him first and foremost. He can never cease marveling over this Holy Lord, who does not tire to forgive. He understands better and better why God must gain such salvation through the cross's suffering and why God made just this to be what the pastor shall witness to, that God gave His only begotten Son. Thus the pastor becomes a true witness. God can say to such pastors what He says here through the prophet: "You are My witness that I have chosen, so that you may know and believe and understand that it is I." The pastor learns this when he himself lives by this Word. He knows that it is so, he believes and he understands. He knows, as only he can know, as he himself has proven. He knows what it is to come to Christ, destitute and poor, and still not be rejected but clothed in the precious clothing and invited to the wedding feast. He believes, in the Christian manner so that he has a steadfast conviction that this Savior both can and will help. He understands that it is God who operates here. He understands why God must operate so, why He must give His only Son, and why nothing else could help the world and me. In this way God makes real witnesses of those whom He has chosen, the witnesses in whose voices one hears that they know what they speak of, and in which one can see that their eyes have really seen this salvation. And yet the whole time they don't speak about themselves and their own experience, but about him who has done all this.

"You are My witnesses, and I am God." So the Lord says now to both of you who stand before His altar today. He is God, who knows all. We can never marvel enough that He chose us and will have us as His witnesses. To give us certainty concerning this inconceivable thing, He gives us the outer, visible call to that which is invisible in the heart and confirms His will through this ordination that happens in His name. Here He says, "You are My witnesses, and I am God." There we have only to say, "Here I am, Lord. As You want, Lord. Yes, Lord, as You will, in everything and at all times as You have said, as You determine, as You find best. Your will be done." Amen.

Ordination Sermon for December 29, 1963

I RECEIVED MERCY,
1 Timothy 1:16

But I received mercy for this reason, that in me, as the foremost, Jesus Christ might display his perfect patience as an example to those who were to believe in him for eternal life.
—1 Timothy 1:16 ESV

It is the old Paul who speaks this way. He is puzzled at how it came to be that he, who had been a blasphemer, persecutor, and assailant could be taken into Christ's ministry and that Christ found him to be trustworthy. He often comes back to this theme: the great wonder that he, contrary to all reason and all probability, would be an apostle of Jesus Christ.

A pastor often has reason to marvel at this too. He will return to this question often in the course of the years. He has reason to do this when he steps into the office too.

How could it happen? Why am I called to this? The more serious a pastor takes this office and Christianity, all the more clearly he knows that he is a sinner like all the others, and accordingly he has to constantly return to God's Word and may constantly see himself in the role. If he is an honest soul, who applies the Word to himself, then he will ever again come under this judgment. He will more and more be convinced that he does not deserve this. He comes to a deeper conviction to concur with Paul's word, that he is the greatest among sinners, a sinner who never learned to keep the two most important commandments, to love his Father in heaven above all things and everyone in his life as much as himself.

Why has He then called me? Why has He placed me to do this that is the greatest and most important thing on earth to do: to preach Christ's

Gospel, to proclaim the forgiveness of sins, to distribute Christ's body and blood, to be a shepherd and teacher for God's congregation.

When Paul marvels at this, he finds no other explanation than God's boundless mercy. But I received mercy, he says, for this reason, that Christ Jesus will display His perfect patience in me first of all. Paul has understood the Gospel. He has understood that it is the escape of forgiveness that we have not deserved. It is given not to the worthy, but the unworthy. God is the one who justifies the ungodly. To carry such a message, it is fitting that such a messenger belongs to the unworthy, those who have not deserved it. Paul knows that he stands there as a living example of this teaching. It is precisely this that he preaches: "For there is no distinction: for all have sinned and fall short of the glory of God, and are justified by his grace as a gift, through the redemption that is in Christ Jesus" (Rom. 3:22–24 ESV).

This is what the pastor will preach, and he shall live by it too. He is a sinner, who lives by the grace of God. But he certainly will not be a sinner that sins by the grace of God. On the contrary, he shall be the first to discipline his old Adam; he is put to a test. When he preaches for others, he can come short of the test, namely, if he applies it to others but not himself, so that he preaches repentance, but he refuses to listen when God's Spirit speaks to him about one of his failings and pet sins, his own comfortableness and self-absorption, his anxiety concerning himself, and his desire to establish himself. But when he applies the Law to himself and stands under its judgment, he may also apply the Gospel and know that he stands forgiven, and all the lovely promises apply to him.

It is this that Paul means when he says that Jesus will let him be a prototype of those who through faith in Him would receive eternal life. Paul knows that people in the future shall find comfort in this, that he, Paul, the persecutor, was an apostle. He can himself find comfort in this when he looks upon those who seem to be hopeless cases. He needs never doubt, he can always say to himself, "If I could be saved, so can they." And he knows that men in the future will come to speak about Paul and think about him and say, "If he could be saved, then so can I."

Paul is right. Countless Christians, among them Martin Luther, have found the deepest comfort from his letters and example. Here they have been able to see before them what it means to be saved by grace.

The pastor will also remember this. He can be something of an example in this too. It is the deepest comfort he can find during the fight with his own old Adam and in his constantly repeated confession of sin. He needs not doubt. If he thinks that he is the worst of sinners, unworthy to be the congregation's leader and shepherd, then he can always comfort himself knowing that God has a particular reason for making such a man a pastor. When God did not choose those in the world who were noble—those who all could be looked up to as some great example, characters without the tiniest blemish, never wavering in their spirit of self-sacrifice, shining and fascinating in their kindness and thoughtfulness for all—but instead He chose completely common sinners, for this reason He would show His mercy on them first and make clear that mercy is for common sinners.

The common sinner can then be a prototype, something that others can have before their eyes and say: yes, this is really Gospel, this is something even for me. So the pastor becomes like Paul a picture of those who would come to believe in Jesus, who justifies sinners, one such faith that makes it so one cannot live without Jesus, a faith that is therefore also real in love.

And it is this we wish for you three who today stand before that altar to be clothed with the holy pastoral office, that you may be such prototypes, men who live by the Gospel you now are sent out with, sinners who stand under the Law and take the confession of sins seriously, who shall pray before God's altar on the congregation's behalf, but pardoned sinners who live by the Gospel and constantly rejoice in this wondrous fact, that Jesus has willed to show His mercy first on us.

Ordination Sermon for May 25, 1964

I PROCLAIM TO YOU WHAT YOU WORSHIP AS UNKNOWN,
Acts 17:23

> The seventeenth chapter of Acts relates that Paul said to the Athenians that he found them to be very religious. For example he fount a temple with the inscription "To the unknown god." And now he says, *"What therefore you worship as unknown, this I proclaim to you."*
> —Acts 17:23 ESV

A Swedish pastor often has reason to say the same. He can say it with the joy that needs to be found in a messenger who brings such great and joyful news.

Certainly, there are skeptics, deniers of God and atheists in our land. But in all the attempts to judge, they make a small minority. The grand majority of the people we meet are religious. They think that there is a God. They pray at times, or maybe every evening. They know that God places certain demands on us. They hope that they will find eternal life. They are, of course, created by God. They have the human heart's capacity to sense the presence of God in His creation. They say, and maybe completely right, that they do their worship in nature. There they perceive the plainest radiance of His glory. They hear His voice in their conscience. Many attempt to follow it uprightly. They too have the knowledge of God that we Christians call the universal revelation, that which is given to all people, because they are God's work.

For this reason they more or less have a fragmentary understanding of Christianity. They have at one time learned the Ten Commandments. They know that Jesus is the world's Savior. They gladly go to church once in a while and often experience it as something solemn and profound.

They place value in the Church's service on Baptism, marriage, and burial. They know that the Church has something to give that no one else can give them.

But they have never understood the tiniest bit of Christianity. They know God's demand in their heart. They are convinced that the way to God is through obedience. If one does what God wants, then one is right with God. For this reason they are a little doubtful as to whether they can really call themselves Christians. They have tried, but unsuccessfully. They have a feeling that they have not lived as they should. They ought to change themselves a little, and then they would be real Christians. But they push the matter off. They don't work on it now. Maybe they comfort themselves thinking that in the end God will be gracious with those who did their best. They aren't quite sure though. So they don't come to the Lord's Supper. They would hardly want or dare to call themselves disciples of Jesus.

Therefore God is often an unknown God. There is so much that is uncertain. One meets so many different opinions. There are many that can be interesting to discuss, but in the end the greater questions remain.

In the midst of this uncertainty, these questions, and this longing, the pastor is set to preach. He has something that these people have not discovered: the real revelation, God's intervention in the world, where He Himself speaks, where He makes Himself known, where He comes down to us in the form of the Son. The greatest is this: that God wants us men to have an insight about the truth, the truth that saves. He wants us to know Him and know who He is. Because He has given us this Word that is not a collection of human opinions, poetic attempts to capture religious feelings, but a real message from another world.

Here the pastor can say, "This God is the one that I proclaim to you." This is the pastor's mission, to speak about Him. To notify. To bring a greeting and a message from God Himself. To say what some lips of men would never be able to say if God Himself had not said it. To help men to know that which no one would be able to discovered, but that God has revealed.

This is what it means to be a servant of the Word. This is what allows even a young pastor to step up boldly. He is not relating his own thoughts. He may not bring out his own life experience. He comes with the Gospel, which means a joyful message that deals with what happened on our earth, and a Word that is said at God's behest.

Perhaps the pastor is called a fanatic. Maybe he hears that there must be other ways and other ideas just as truthful. He can never agree with this. If he did, he would deny his Lord Christ. Christ is truth, not part of the truth, and not one among many thoughtworthy truths. For this reason the disciple says, "Lord to whom shall I go? You have the words of eternal life." In the same manner the pastor says before all objections: "Whom shall I believe? I believe in Jesus Christ, God's only begotten Son, My Lord." The pastor who so dares to trust in his Lord, he will see that men really listen. He will be able to see how many there are who are thankful to have a firm Word that does not come from men. But before all he shall experience how needed and longed for it is that the Gospel be preached also in our time. He shall see how the eyes of men open and that they understand the Gospel. They understand that they are not alone in their failure with the Law. They understand that this does not shut them out from God. They understand that the basis for all of Christianity is forgiveness. They dare to come to the Lord's Supper. In their lives one begins to see the calm changes that happen where God's Spirit has His dwelling in men.

Today we will wish you who are to be new brothers in the office that which we wish for ourselves, that we all shall be able to preach the Gospel with the joy of a messenger who comes with something new, something unknown, something important, and often longed after to men who well know God and know that they need Him but who still do not understand the greatest He has done and the most He has to give. Here we can again say with Paul, "But how are they to call on him in whom they have not believed? And how are they to believe in him of whom they have never heard? And how are they to hear without someone preaching? And how are they to preach unless they are sent? As it is written, 'How beautiful are the feet of those who preach the good news!'" (Rom. 10:14–15 ESV).

This is our desire today for you who are now sent to preach by ordination into the holy pastoral office and for us who already stand in the same ministry: to step into this service shall be lovely for us and for others, so that we may be such messengers who proclaim peace and come with the joyful message.

Ordination Sermon for December 28, 1964

OUT OF EGYPT,
Matthew 2:15

Out of Egypt I called my son.
—Matthew 2:15 ESV

These words have a particular connection with this day. On this day, the Church has long commemorated the martyrs in Bethlehem, the innocent children who were able to give their lives so that the baby Jesus would live, He who would then give His life so that the world would live. In the narration of the infanticide in Bethlehem, we also read of the flight to Egypt and about how God, when the danger had subsided, called His Son back. It is written that this happened so that it would be fulfilled, what was said of the Lord through the prophet: "Out of Egypt I called my son" (Matt. 2:15 ESV).

Today, this word has something to say to you who are being ordained to the pastoral office and to us who have already been entrusted with it. Perhaps though, it is not immediately apparent. God's Word is just that way. Under its surface is concealed a depth that no one ever fully plumbs. Every little word is included in a greater connection that one is never completely finished with.

How is it for the evangelist that something so edifying, something the prophet Hosea once said about Israel, now applies to Jesus? Naturally, first because he again confirmed that all Holy Scripture witnessed to the Messiah, Jesus, and that the whole of Israel's history, the Law, and the temple worship were full of types that point to Him. But there was something more. There is a comfort and a Gospel in this, that God had called His Son out of Egypt. According to Israel, Egypt was the land of bondage, but it was also the rich and mighty land, the land of fleshpots, the land that was full of wisdom, of fortunetellers and secret arts, of powerful temples and noteworthy creations of highly developed techniques. Egypt was far and away beyond Israel in all that we consider civilization to be. That God once had carried His people out of Egypt, that meant that He chose those in the world who were weak and despised and let the strong be shamed. He showed that His foolishness was wiser than man's wisdom and His weakness stronger than the strength of man, as Paul speaks. He showed that the Word, which He gave to His people, was more than all the glory the world had to offer. Just as He triumphed over all of Egypt's wisdom and all the pharaoh's glory at that time, so now He once again shows that He has carried His plans through, despite Herod the dictator and all else that then marveled the world: the wisdom of the Greeks, and the power of the Romans. He triumphed by something that was and is hidden before the wise and clever, yet is the power of God for salvation to all who believe. "Out of Egypt I called my son." This means that out of the spiritual Egypt, out of the security with the world's fleshpots, away from the wisdom that wants to have guarantees for everything, I have called My people, My Son, and My Church. My kingdom is not of this world. For this reason it cannot be conquered.

And now we begin to understand what this word has to say to a pastor.

Maybe it speaks very personally to him. "Out of Egypt, I called my Son." It applies to many pastors today, that God called them out of the Egypt of atheism and materialism. At home there may be no one who would think about the pastoral call, least of all for himself. But God called on His Son and nudged Him to leave Egypt, out to a ministry that many in our surroundings look at with amazement or dismissal. But just as Moses, he who was instructed in all the wisdom of Egypt, kept Christ's disgrace as a greater treasure than Egypt's treasure, so it is an honor and privilege for us to serve Christ, rather than choose a different path that looks better in the eyes of the world.

Out of Egypt is perhaps also called the pastor that comes from a Christian home where one prays and hopes that he should take this path. For him it means that he is a servant of a Word that the world rejects, a message that cannot be proven, a manner of life that does not stand high in the culture of Egypt, where one coldly calculates how to get as much pleasure as possible here and now, as much income or power during the short earthly life that one considers his only sure asset. A Christian is called out, out of the situation, to bear his shame. It is his privilege.

Also when a pastor looks at his congregation, this word becomes a Gospel and a promise. The pastor looks at his confirmands. He notices how little study they do at home, how little they understand of what Christianity is, how hard it must be for them to take the Christian path when their studies are over. It can seem completely hopeless. But then the evangelist says, "Out of Egypt, I called my son." God has always retrieved His people from this powerful, overly courageous, cocksure Egypt. He still does it today. The pastor looks at many who do not enter the sanctuary to hear the Word. He notices their obvious security. They think of themselves as normal, as modern, according to the changing times. But again the prophet says, "Out of Egypt, I called My son." The people who seem fettered by the rich and arrogant Egypt, the hand of God carries them out. And God's own Son, He who was tempted in everything like us and knows all our difficulties, He Himself made the exodus symbolically as a child and in a very real way when He as a grown man met all these temptations in the form of a Hellenistic culture that ruled on the other side of the lake in his homeland of Galilee and that reigned within the hearts of men even in Capernaum and Jerusalem. He also met this power and these temptations. Therefore He can have compassion on us who are now pressured by them. He has overcome them. Therefore He can carry us out of Egypt.

May He then carry us out. First and foremost us pastors who receive the call to go to the front, who guide and shepherd the flock, but also our congregations, who are His people. "It is he who made us, and we are his; we are his people, and the sheep of his pasture" (Ps. 100:3 ESV).

Ordination Sermon for May 25, 1965

I BOW MY KNEES BEFORE THE FATHER,
Ephesians 3:14-15

For this reason I bow my knees before the Father, from whom every family in heaven and on earth is named.
—Ephesians 3:14–15 ESV

We are all reminded that it is Paul who bows his famous knees to the Father in the third chapter of Ephesians. It is a prayer for the congregation. It is a prayer that every pastor can pray from the day he is ordained to the office until he sits old, gray, and powerless and does not have the strength to do anything more for his beloved Church than pray for it.

Today, my young brothers, when you are ordained to this office, and we who stand around you think back on our own ordination day, we will tarry over these words that are at the entrance to the prayers, and that can be used as a portal to the pastor's prayers for himself and his congregation, for the work of his office and the whole of his life as a servant of the Word: "For this reason I bow my knees before the Father, from whom every family in heaven and on earth is named" (Eph. 3:14–15 ESV).

It is before the Father I bow my knees. That I call Him Father, this is not just a metaphor, not just some poor attempt to borrow an earthly concept and an earthly experience in order to attempt expression of that which is not easily expressed. Men will, of course, declare all our statements about God vain attempts to say what cannot be said, or maybe only some empty projection of human need, human experiences of fatherly authority and the security of childhood, out in a space that in reality is empty.

But here the Bible tells us it is the opposite, that the only reason we can say something about God is because God reproduced something of His being down here on earth and lets us see it as in a mirror. God's invisible being, His eternal power and divine glory, have been visible since the creation of the world. They can be understood through His work. They shine through all of creation, and it is man's mark of nobility that he can perceive it. In the same manner, some of God's being shines through in all that deserves the name father on earth. God has created the relationship between parents and children, and everything of which that consists. He has given it a particularity, a task, a possibility, and when some of this is realized, then it mirrors some of God's being. In all that father means on heaven and earth, in everything that gives basis for the name, in all fatherly love, the tenderness of a father, fatherly care, fatherly worry, and fatherly joy, some of God's being is mirrored. As He is in relation to the Son, so He is in His relationship to His children on earth. We know that it is only a matter of a glimmer, something we conceive in glimpses and capture as a reflection. And yet, it is a way for God to make Himself known, a piece of His revelation. And He has given this revelation to every generation and to all people in the same manner as the revelation in nature and conscience that He has declared and confirmed in the revelation of His Word. So He is. We know it, for He has Himself said it. As a father has compassion on his children, so the Lord has compassion on those who fear Him. Your Father in heaven, He knows that you need all this. The Father Himself loves you.

And now I begin to understand what it means to be able to bow one's knees before the Father. When the pastor does this and prays for his congregation, he speaks to the Father, who, as a matter of fact, is already out there among the people, who holds all creation in His hand, who lives and works in a hundred ways even in the natural life, in the love of parents and the trust of children, in loyalty and concern. It can never be hopeless to work in a world that God holds in His hand and where His being is mirrored in so many ways. Men may try to get away by whatever means, they may appear crazy and possessed by an insane desire to push God away at any price; still he is there among them. He is the Father who gives them their lives and who still seeks after them. It can never be hopeless to work in such a world. And then, He is also our Father. He knows all, knows what we need, long before we say it. We are reminded of Luther's explanation of the Lord's Prayer: "God desires with these words to invite us to believe, that He is our true Father, and we are His true children, so that we should ask Him boldly and with all confidence as dear children ask their dear Father."

It is also a good order for a pastor who prays for his congregation, for his own family, for his neighbors and friends, for his students and his elders, for the entire great crowd that fills page after page of the congregation's record book. It is before this Father he bows his knees, before Him from whom all that father means in heaven and earth has its name. Therefore he dares to say, "Abba, Father, for You everything is possible." Therefore he can also say, "Then not as I will but as You will." No one can know better; no one can grieve more faithfully; no one can deal more certainly than the Father of all that father means. He is the Father of mercy and the God of all comfort.

This is the entrance through which a pastor may enter his office on his own day of ordination, and then day after day in his work. And whether we now begin our first day's work as pastors tomorrow or our ten thousandth, we will bow our knees before this Father, who will be able to do infinitely much more than we can pray or think. To Him belongs the glory in the Church and in Christ Jesus, all generations forever and ever. Amen.

Ordination Sermon for December 29, 1965

THE LORD COMES TO GIVE YOU UNDERSTANDING IN EVERYTHING,
2 Timothy 2:7

In the second chapter of Second Timothy, Paul writes a few words to his young brother in the office, his student and disciple. These words are the greatest promise that we pastors have received, without which we would dare not to be pastors. This promise says, *"Think over what I say, for the Lord will give you understanding in everything."*

—2 Timothy 2:7 ESV

Just before this, Paul spoke about the great mission that comes from Christ and shall be given continuously till the end of time. "What you have heard from me in the presence of many witnesses entrust to faithful men who will be able to teach others also" (2 Tim. 2:2 ESV).

It is this mission that shall be given anew today to yet another proprietor. It is a mission to instruct others. What can seem more presumptuous than to instruct others about God in matters of the faith when one is perhaps much younger than the people he instructs? It would be pure presumptuousness if the mission were not given by God Himself and the message His own. The skill to instruct others about God does not come through one's own intelligence. What is it Paul says? "Not that we are sufficient in ourselves to claim anything as coming from us, but our sufficiency is from God, who has made us competent to be ministers of a new covenant, not of the letter but of the Spirit. For the letter kills, but the Spirit gives life" (2 Cor. 3:5–6 ESV).

The first thing we have to do in order that the Lord shall be able to give us understanding in everything is also to listen to that which comes from God, to really make us faithful to the whole of this message that is given to us in God's Word. It is here we have to seek the complete truth about which we are to instruct others. Therefore a true pastor prays just like the pious in the Old Testament: "Give me understanding, so that I can know Your witness. Give me understanding according to Your Word. Give me understanding, so that I can learn Your command."

But understanding in everything. It means something more. It does not mean just knowledge concerning God's Word, faithfulness concerning the Bible. It also means what the fathers called insight. The same word Paul uses here is closest in meaning and is also translated with "insight into the mystery of Christ" (Eph. 3:4), and it is something more than knowledge. It is not only understanding in the meaning of good human judgment. It is a question about an ability to conceive and understand that which is completely hidden from the wise and clever. Here it means in highest degree that the Lord shall give us understanding. Only He can do it. And it is that which He does when He lets the Word work on our hearts, and we let Him carry out His work. Then a man wins insight into God's Word. He may understand to grasp the actuality, the reality, the concrete and living meaning of such words as sin, guilt, grace, justification, and sanctification. No one ever conceives the meaning without standing under God's judgment and grace himself. But when one does that, he receives understanding in these things, an experience and knowledge that makes it possible for us to instruct others. This is most important, for otherwise the whole of a pastor's life, if not our preaching, shall be empty words and nice clichés. But he who goes to God's school receives understanding in everything that touches faith, a completely deeper and richer understanding. He comes to receive an experience that Paul calls "all the riches of full assurance of understanding and the knowledge of God's mystery, which is Christ, in whom are hidden all the treasures of wisdom and knowledge" (Col. 2:2–3 ESV). One of the mysteries in the art of being able to stand and preach year after year without tiring oneself, and without tiring those who hear, is to be able to gather up all the treasures of wisdom and knowledge from Christ's inexhaustible wells.

Understanding in everything. That includes one more thing also: a good understanding in matters of this world, in how to handle a person who threatens to commit suicide, to meet a noisy confirmand, to lead an assembly with many antagonists. Even in things like this God gives a good understanding when people love Him, when they are willing to sacrifice their own prestige for the sake of the matter, when they are careful with themselves, their words and steps, but looking over and forgiving when it comes to others. Even this is something that the Lord gives when one first seeks His kingdom and His righteousness. The Scriptures have much to say about such understanding in everything that makes one know how one shall answer whoever, how one shall behave among those who stand outside and do not share our faith but seek constantly new reasons to attack and critique. The art of taking every opportunity in deed, to know when one shall be silent and pray for God's time, even this understanding comes as a gift from the Lord, when one takes His Word seriously and uses it to judge over his heart's intents and thoughts.

So we thank the Lord, who gave us this promise for our office and pray to Him for grace to be so faithful to Him and His Word that He can let it be fulfilled in our poor lives and our humble service.

Ordination Sermon for May 24, 1966

I AM SENDING THE PROMISE OF MY FATHER UPON YOU,
Luke 24:49

And behold, I am sending the promise of my Father upon you.
—Luke 24:49 ESV

It was Christ's promise to the apostles, given to them right before the ascension. It was a promise that they well needed. They should go out and preach the Gospel to all creation. Of themselves, they had no resources for this absurd mission. They were an exceedingly small minority among their people. They had no political influence and no powerful patrons. They were hated by their compatriots. The Romans despised them. The Greeks considered them a laughingstock. How would they be able to get respect for the absurd message they would now preach?

Essentially, being a pastor is always a bit absurd. We are sent out to preach a reality whose existence can never be demonstrated the way one demonstrates the world's realities. We are to proclaim events that never happened before or after on our earth, something absolutely unique, events that go beyond all normal experience. We cannot make it any more probable by our own sharp thoughts or the experience that a long life gives. It can be entrusted to one who is much younger than his congregation. It can seem preposterous at such a young age to say such weighty things and come with a message that demands to be heard and received even by one who has great knowledge and more experience in other areas. Being a pastor is a bit absurd.

But the Savior said, "And behold, I am sending the promise of my Father upon you" (Luke 24:49 ESV). No one knew better than the Savior what a hard mission He laid upon His apostles. He never made it a secret that they would be met by unrest, enmity, and opposition. But yet He commanded them to go out and promised them power to be His witnesses. He would send them what the Father had promised.

This that we have been promised is the Holy Spirit. For the apostles it meant that God with His Spirit would lead them into all truth, reminding them of what Christ said, to teach them rightly and preach it rightly. He shall give them the right thoughts and the right orders, so that the message would not be distorted but reach men with a word from Christ's own lips.

This means that we possess this word and this message in the apostolic Scriptures. We are freed from all doubt about what we really will preach, that which is truth, that which really happened, who this Christ is and what His life, death, and resurrection mean for us today. But it also means that we have the promise of God's help to understand it rightly, to apply it rightly to ourselves, and to preach it rightly for others.

"And behold, I am sending the promise of my Father upon you" (Luke 24:49 ESV). No one can need this promise more than a pastor. Nothing can give him more comfort and boldness. "I am sending the promise of my Father upon you," Christ says. When He says that this is His will and promises that He will do this, when I dare to enter this office and take this responsibility upon myself, I have the Father's promise—that which in our translation is translated "the promise of my Father." "The promise of my Father" is also the name of the Holy Spirit. It is a wonderful name for Him who is also called the Comforter and the Paraclete. He is not only the power but the power that we have been promised. He is not only the Spirit of truth but the Spirit who according to God's promise shall lead us into all truth. He is not only the Comforter but my Comforter, He who I have been promised. He is the promise of the Father, given by the God and Father of our Lord Jesus Christ, He is my security. Because I have this promise, I dare take this step.

Because we also pray at our ordination, "Veni Sancte Spiritus!" "Oh You, Holy Spirit, come to us." And this prayer must remain in the pastor's heart if he truly shall be able to manage his office. This absurd mission can only be carried out in the Spirit's power. Accordingly, to a true sermon the Holy Spirit shall be able to give His Amen. And when a true pastor knows the Spirit's reproof, comfort, or leading in his heart, he says, "Amen."

Because today we also pray the Pentecost hymn over a thousand years old:

> Come Holy Spirit, Lord God,
> Enter our hearts, give us courage,
> Grant us Your holy grace
> And be with us in word and deed. Amen.

Ordination Sermon for December 28, 1966

AT YOUR WORD I WILL LET DOWN THE NETS,
Luke 5:5

And Simon answered, "Master, we toiled all night and took nothing! But at your word I will let down the nets."
—Luke 5:5 ESV

We remember these words. Peter dropped them one time on a fishing trip that became his call to the ministry of the Word. The fishing trip itself was a picture of the ministry. For this reason, the story has always had so much to say to them who are God's servants in the pastoral office.

This word says something essential both at the beginning of the office and in the continuation through the years.

"At your word . . ." (Luke 5:5 ESV). It is the basis upon which we dare to enter the office. Peter is saying that he would never have done this on his own initiative. Had the Lord not stood there and directly commanded him, he would not have cast out the nets. So it is also the right attitude regarding the pastor's office. When one enters it, he says: "At Your word, Lord." This is not something that a man makes up for himself or decides on for himself. Should one measure it according to human measures, then it appears just as absurd and hopeless as Peter thought it was to cast out the nets one more time. It doesn't makes sense to shrewd reason to consecrate your life to proclaim that a man who was executed some two thousand years ago rose again from the dead and lives and is always our Lord.

It is just as unreasonable today as it was in the days of the apostles. In order to do something like this, one must be able to say, "At Your word, Lord." Only if one knows the Lord and has received His command can one dare embark upon such adventure. But then one cannot refrain. You cannot escape. A man knows that He is the one who determines and not one's self. One understands the apostle's word, "Woe to me if I do not proclaim the Gospel."

"At your word . . ." It contains yet another reminder for those who enter the pastoral office. His Word not only commands me to go out, His Word follows me. It tells me what I should preach. I can say before each new task, "At Your word, Lord. It is not me who speaks here. It is You. It is not me who shall think through what needs to be said now. I shall seek out Your Word." One corrupts the entire holy office, one makes it absurdly hard for himself, and his hearers miss the most essential if one does not let his Lord's Word be that which determines everything, answers every question, and gives me the message that I am to carry forward, without being embarrassed by it and without fearing the consequences. Therefore, we may not replace this word, this norm, "at your word," for some modern surrogate. We cannot reinterpret it, blot it out, and say that we must invite men to Christendom in modern forms. Let us instead simply and faithfully listen to our Lord and then say, "At Your word, Lord . . ."

But there is something more in this word of Peter, something he himself could hardly have known at the moment but possibly thought of later on. There are so many of the Lord's words that become more profound and take on new meaning as one continues in his Lord's service for a few years or a few decades. This is one of them. This day is the first day in the pastoral office for some of us who stand in front of God's altar in the evening. Some have already had more than sixty years in the ministry. But this word applies to us all: "At your word." Maybe, one learns to understand this all the more and deeper when one can say as Peter, "Master, we toiled all night and took nothing!" (Luke 5:5 ESV). This experience belongs to the pastoral office too. One sows, and some falls on the path, some on the stony ground, some among the thorns. There are times when one thinks like the prophet: "I have labored in vain; I have spent my strength for nothing and vanity" (Isa. 49:4 ESV). A fisher of men I would have been, but how few I have caught. How many times have I not sat up and worked into the late hours of the night to have a full and well-grounded message to come with. And the result? I have caught nothing.

"But"—and here it is a big "but," as every pastor has learned in the Lord's service. "But at Your word I will let down the nets."

"But at your word . . ." Despite everything, without questioning, after setbacks in the past and improbabilities just now, at Your word, only at Your word, Lord. This is sufficient basis to dare to take the first unfamiliar steps in the office, sufficient basis to continue through the years, sufficient basis to keep going when your faith is tested to the extreme.

"At Your word, Lord . . ." It can also be placed as a slogan and mission statement for the holy pastoral office that shall be given to new keepers. Whether we stand in the beginning of the ministry or near the end, we may bow humbly before Him who is Lord of the office. He who is called to it and works in it says, "Lord, we are not worthy. Lord, we won't do. Lord, we are miserable tools. But at Your word we still do it, still go out, still sow in the rocks, still cast our nets. If You can use us, then do so. If You fill the nets, so we praise You for Your unmerited grace. If You let us work without seeing the result, then it is still a grace to be able to stand in Your service." So we will engage in the work. So we will continue to work. At Your word, Lord.

Ordination Sermon in Växjö on December 17, 1972

MY WITNESSES IN THIS WORLD,
Isaiah 43:12

> "'You are my witnesses,' declares the LORD, 'and I am God.'"
> —Isaiah 43:12 ESV

So God tells His people Israel and His Church. However, these words don't apply to us in the same way they were meant at the time. God spoke to the captives in Babylon, to this remnant of the nation that in the world's eyes were "deeply despised, abhorred by the nation, the servant of rulers." In somewhat the same way that today the Church is considered by many to be a dying remnant that has no future, so the enemies of Israel thought that the Jews and their faith were finished. Their God had said that it was He who chose Israel. He had determined that they should be His vessel for the salvation of the world. Now, the naysayers scornfully reckon that the world is steered by very different realities: power, money, and armament. But God spoke to His beaten people, "worm Jacob, men of Israel," and said, "You are my witnesses . . . and I am God" (Isa. 43:12 ESV).

He says the same to us—to you who are now ordained to be His witnesses in the midst of the world where so many believe that the future is determined by completely different realities than God's Word and that God's will and God's people are a remnant that do not need to reckoned with.

Today He says the very same thing He said then: "You are my witnesses." Witnesses—but to what?

The witness to that "I have said it." God has spoken to this world and God speaks through the very same word. "I declared and saved and proclaimed." The world has always said it was a fantasy. Now it is finished.

But God's work is carried through just as He had said before. "Bring out the people who are blind, yet have eyes," says the Lord (Isa. 43:8 ESV). All people assemble. Who among them can declare this? Men scornfully smile—and God carries His work through. He saved His people Israel out of Babel and brought them back. He sends His Messiah. People crucified Him, and again His enemies scorned triumphantly. But God raised Him from the dead. The world looked with scorn at this fantasy that preached something so absurd as a crucified Savior. But God gave His Gospel victory also over the critical Greeks and scornful Romans. God lives.

And now we stand here as His witnesses in our time to say this with boldness and joy, and men may believe or not. But this is precisely what God has given men to testify to today: "I, I am the LORD, and besides Me there is no savior. Before Me no god was formed, nor shall there be any after Me. You are My servants, them whom I have chosen. You are My witnesses, and I am God."

It is fantastical to witness in such a world and in such a time as ours. A world where men oscillate between being filled with titanic arrogance—believing they are able to do anything with their technical skill and computers, who will manipulate man and play God—and then being filled with dissolution and despair thinking all is a failure, that everything will fall to pieces, and we will have to begin all over again from the beginning. Or maybe a disappointment and a feeling of meaninglessness so deep and so typical of this day and age that it has been given its own name. They call it frustration and alienation. Yet in the midst of all this, the Lord says: "I have told you before. If you do not have faith, you shall not have peace." Life has a meaning and a purpose: that we shall be God's children. This meaning is available to everyone because God Himself has atoned for all the world's sins through His Son's death—what God promised the fathers that He has done. And what has happened before will happen again. Christ will come again. This world goes to its end; the time is short. We wait for His promise, new heavens and a new earth where we will live righteous lives. The Lord is near.

For all this we are now sent out to witness. You who stand here to be ordained to the holy pastoral office, I congratulate you. It is a glorious mission. Many think that we live in a time of dusk and in a world fallen in sin. We who are His witnesses know the truth. The night is advanced and the day is near. We are placed as watchers, to cry out that the day dawns, that the morning stars go up, that the true light already shines, and that it is glorious to live. By God is the light, the power, the means and the grace, by Him who now says, "You are my witnesses . . . and I am God."

ESSAYS

HOW THE *SEELSORGER* CARES FOR HIS OWN SOUL

Course for Father Confessors IX: 1.

The priest is just another man . . . It is so true, so true. And then so false.

Certainly priests are men, with the whole of the sinful inheritance and all the temptations that other humans are afflicted with: the same sexuality, the same inclination for self-assertion, the same desire to dodge responsibility, the same cowardice before self-assured repudiation, and the same inertia before the Word of God. A true priest knows more than well that he is only a man. If he has an objection to this characterization, it is more than likely that he is not just a man but an unusually great sinner.

And still the priest is not just a man. He is a person, who has been given a very difficult and huge position of responsibility. Though he is a common sinner, he is called to be a proclaimer of God's Word, a herald of the Lord, a shepherd and leader of God's people. He has received a charge that brings with it very great and unusual possibilities, as well as very difficult and peculiar temptations. He is a man who has been entrusted with much and must wrestle with much. He is a man with an entirely different responsibility. Through him the message of salvation is to go out into the world. If he fails, it affects many, and it affects them not only with earthly misfortune but also with serious danger to the soul. If the shepherd is struck so must the flock scatter. In all this, the priest is by no means just another man. He is a person with a responsibility that is far and above the normal measure of responsibility.

Therefore, the priest has a particular responsibility for his own soul. It is not merely a concern for himself. He needs to continually pray with the psalmist: Let not those who hope in you be put to shame through me.

Strangely enough, it may now help the *seelsorger* with his particular situation if he looks at himself for a moment as just another man and compares the points in which he is like all the others. This is what we are going to now compare in seven points, where the priest's similarity with others can be seen and what the particular dangers and the particular treasures of his position are, and thereby also learn something of the curer of soul's care for his own soul.

1. Even the *Seelsorger* Has an Old Adam.

A pious old woman in our district was once taught to say, "Yes, behold, priests do not have the same sinful inheritance…." It takes quite a bit charity to say so, maybe much blindness too. The fighting, the jokes, and all our slander show better. Even many of the peaceful in the land, who are the last to judge or criticize, have with sad eyes seen how far the Old Adam sticks his head out in a priest. It may be useful to look at a common caricature of a priest. He is fat. No one sees that he disciplines his body and subdues it. He is a little pompous. No one hears that he has come to serve and be a servant to everyone. He loves good food and is afraid of bad weather. No one fathoms that life for him is Christ or that his heart burns with the zeal of God.

Just as the Old Adam does not die in Baptism, so he survives ordination also. If he gets some time to himself, he can get along wonderfully well in the cassock. If he is not subdued, bound, and crucified, he will gradually take control of the whole administration of the office. He does it by writing off what fits him least. Usually it is visiting the sick, seeking out the care of souls, and continually making new attempts to reach out to people. Instead, he leaves the worldly men in peace, retreating back into the administration of the office's safe spheres, and gives glory to God alone on behalf of the servants in sufficiently polished sermons. He harvests well-deserved recognition for his municipal contributions. And finally the old Adam is carried to the grave while the congregation sincerely mourns and speaks of its thankfulness for his meaningful contributions to the community, as if he had done absolutely nothing wrong. The old Adam can be a difficult troublemaker. During meetings and in church councils he happily disrupts with confusion. Between brothers in the office, he wakes envy and feud. He schemes with every choice, and he doesn't forget old grudges easily.

Therefore, a priest must also work out his own salvation with fear and trembling. He must keep after his old Adam. When he meets opposition, he must recognize that his wrath is not simply holy. He must test his zeal to see if it isn't hiding thirst for power or desire for vengeance in it. He must lay down all his principles before God with the humble question of whether or not he possibly misuses them as justification of the flesh. It can be cowardice and laziness that I do not want to do some youth activity or will not go to people uncalled. It can be flight from God that pushes me into new associations and hunts after new and more effective forms when actually all that is needed is to learn a different style of preaching God's Word. It can be pure pride that makes a priest attend to everything himself, rather than fostering laymen to take over what can be taken over. The old Adam needs to be unmasked in everything: in the anxious worries of the missing brother in the office, who so likes to poke about in other's small scandals and chat about their mistakes in the false resignation that says that I have done mine if only I have preached God's undefiled Word on Sunday; or in the indifferent orthodoxy that tells the few listeners gathered together that they will surely be lost if they do not repent. But he says it in such a careless and indifferent manner that it makes absolutely no difference how it is received, only that it is dutifully said.

If a priest lets God's Holy Spirit keep after his old Adam as perpetually and as painfully as His dispute with the flesh, with its laziness and indolence, its desire for prestige and ambition, its schadenfreude and filth, then original sin itself can be a resource. This can at least do the priest the favor of furnishing him with perpetually new examples of the flesh's activities, perpetually new illustrations for the Scripture's word of Law, which is in our members and makes us to toil under the law of sin. This is no small favor. If one only speaks in universalities about sin, the parishioners will only be amused by everything they did at the dance pavilion on Saturday or in their youth, or they may sleep. But they begin to hear and possibly take it to heart if one suddenly begins to speak in another sense about their home, the way one answers the telephone, or that we are by nature such that we would rather speak a half an hour with an indifferent person about indifferent things than ten minutes with God in prayer.

Even the priest has an old Adam. It must either be crucified daily, or it will come to rule. In theory we all know how it ought to be. Then in knowledge of this, blessed is the one who does it.

2. Even the *Seelsorger* Needs God's Word.

Who doesn't know this? Who would deny this?

To be quite honest, there are priests who live as if they do not know this. Their lives deny it, for instance when they are on vacation. It is a painful observation of pious parishioners in our tourist districts that one or another summer sunbathing priest skips the High Mass. There are pastors whose Bibles are noticeably little used. The pericopes are diligently used, but not the Bible. In such a case, one can seriously suspect that the Word applies to others but that the priest for his own part thinks that "he can do without it." Then there is the great and common temptation of the *seelsorger*'s own soul. This temptation follows us all. We are tempted to apply the Word to others, even when we read the Bible diligently. We find good conversation starters, practical illustrations for next Sunday's office, valuable ideas for the homiletical treatment of old well-known texts. But we experience no sting in the heart, and we seek not the forgiveness of sins. For this reason, the priest too must seek first the kingdom of God and His righteousness in his Bible reading. Certainly, if that is done, everything else will come to him also. Before the Word he must, first and foremost, be a completely common person, not a preacher. When one pursues his Bible study in order to base a sermon, then the thought of the message will step into the foreground. But he must also read the Bible as a common parishioner, for his own upbuilding, for rebuking, for reparation, and for fostering in righteousness, in order to express the matter as Paul does when he warns Timothy to hold fast to the Holy Scriptures he has known since his childhood.

If one does not approach the Word in this manner, it can be fatal for the proclamation in the end. The Word is able not only to save but also to obdurate and harden. If one constantly hears it again and again and yet does not give it room in his heart, letting it both judge and give grace, then it makes the heart harder.

3. Even a *Seelsorger* Needs to Be Converted.

To be converted has always been hard. And it does not get any easier when one lives in a church, where the priest's office is a respected and well-paid social institution, connected with a good deal of historical romanticism, a well-kept parsonage, and a secure future and where the way to the office follows close to exclusively secular studies in a free academic world, which along with much good also contains a great deal of intrigue, gossip, and a flippant manner of dealing with all that is sacred. There is a very great possibility that he will entrench his heart behind theological excuses. He may shun Free Church–type awakening techniques and un-Lutheran pietism and avoid asking the questions, "Am I rightly converted to God? Have I a part in my Savior?"

If the priest is sent to a good congregation, it may happen that they will convert him. But he has a much greater chance of going to a district where very little reminds him of conversion's importance. It is of all circumstances surest that he takes the matter in his own hands—or better, lays this matter in God's hands and prays about a true conversion and about a life of daily renewed repentance. But a right relationship to the Word he does not have. The Law is powerless when it is not received as God's Law, and the Gospel has nothing to say if it may not speak as a sure word from God's own lips, well worth being received. It is precisely the same for daily repentance. It is so easy for a priest to quit meaning anything concrete with his confession of sins, to stop testing his relationship with his wife, his cantor, or his nearest brother in the office and therefore also stop confessing real sins and being willing to make up for them.

4. Even a *Seelsorger* Needs the Support of an External Order.

The external order may not be disregarded, neither under the plea of the demand for intimacy and sincerity. This applies to all of the congregation's life. One shall not quit going to the church because one is forced to do it. One shall not quit bowing his head in the church pew because one often calls irrelevant things to mind. One shall not quit table prayers because it perpetually threatens to become a routine experience.

It is in the same manner with the *seelsorger*. He can think that he has much to do with God's Word and so many reasons to pray that he does not need to take it so seriously with the rest of his devotional habits. It is a dangerous temptation. As a matter of fact, he needs much resoluteness to hold fast to a particular order for his devotion and follow through with it despite all difficulties. Otherwise, hurry and haste come to choke out Word and prayer from his life. First, the many worries and obligations encroach upon the devotions. Then the priest thinks about his approaching sermon, about the troublesome letter he must write, on all the telephone conversations he can't forget. He may bring them up in prayer—and this is not a bad idea. Greater thoughts and persistent feelings draw him before God's face and turn into prayer. But that should not be the end of it. There is so much more that the priest ought to pray about. There are other things he needs to call for in prayer. Therefore, it is also very important to have firm order, not the least for prayer, in the form of a prayer book and a prayer list. Many who during this last decade have used the daily hours have trouble imagining what it would have been like without its help in their prayer life, in all the unrest and constant haste that so often fills our consciousness to the brim.

It does no harm to give one's daily devotion a firm position in the day's schedule, even so firm that the family's other members know about it. It is helpful when devotions can be done in peace. When one is tempted, it helps to run away from it.

5. Even a *Seelsorger* Needs Holy Communion.

Does it need to be said that the pastor needs Holy Communion? Just as often if not more often than laypeople? There are cases where it needs to be said. Pious people in our districts have often wondered how their priests seem to have done so well without going to communion. The nicest have thought that it must mean the priests are particularly holy. The less pious have drawn the conclusion that Communion can hardly be as much of a needed means of grace as the priest said during the Communion address.

Since we have received the possibility for self-Communion, the greatest external hindrance for the priest's Communion has disappeared. By this I only mean that a priest ought to as a rule receive Communion himself when he distributes it to others. I have the experience that one is blessed by it, even when the external circumstances have been unusually hasty and pressing. Just as one is blessed by prayer and the reading of God's Word even when one cannot do it in such peace and tranquility as one would have desired.

6. Even a *Seelsorger* Has Need of Confession.

He shares all the same reasons as laymen. He needs it to help him become clear about his own standing before God. In our district it was normal for the young priests to "be puzzled instructors" and seek simple soul care from some more experienced brother in the office, just like the parishioners. The priest needs this also in order to help fight his old Adam and come to the right understanding concerning the difficulties that perpetually arise between brothers in the office and parishioners. He needs it as help against his spiritual laziness and his own neglect in the use of the means of grace. He needs it very particularly when he has lost his own peace in some other trap that the soul's enemy set before him.

It can be hard for a priest to find a *seelsorger*. But he may not be overly particular and fastidious—as little as a laymen ought to be. Even the priest may be reminded that the office and power of the keys are there despite all personal weaknesses. And though it be ever so hard for him, he still ought to go to his bishop.

And so then finally,

7. Even a *Seelsorger* Has a Merciful Savior, Who Never Fails to Forgive.

This may be the most important thing he needs to be reminded of. This applies to the *seelsorger* and his own soul. It is dangerous for a priest to forget that he needs forgiveness. It is even more dangerous for him to forget that he can receive forgiveness and that he has it on account of Jesus. Serious and diligent priests know so well that much has been entrusted to them, and that much will be demanded of them. Therefore, it can be very risky to hold out. One may place great demands on himself, and one knows that God places one much greater. One is ashamed to come with his petty and small failures, with the nuisances and humiliating common details, the inability of the heart to clear up small conflicts with warm, loving generosity while getting worked up over another's sharp humor.

In this situation lies the temptation to botch it up even more. One speaks to God in ceremonial terms. The prayer may be liturgical. One confesses sins and does it in common terms, gliding past the real sins. Here confession can be a great help. There one is forced to speak concretely.

But there is another temptation: to not trust, to stay in the feeling of wariness, failure, and self-contempt. This is not God's purpose when He lets His Word revise our thoughts, words, and deeds. Just as it is certain that there is real sin in our poor lives, it is certain that there is real forgiveness that we receive on account of Jesus. Therefore shall the last, the fundamental, and the dominating factor in our life be joy—the joy that you are in the Lord always. Serve the Lord with joy. This is not the least important for the priest, who here on earth stands in the forecourts of heaven, placed by the door through which he continually distributes heaven's gifts to his congregation. For this reason, he can always be joyful in the Lord, not because of himself, not because of his congregation, not over great successes, but because of his Lord, because of the great Savior who does not fail to forgive and who lets every day be a new day of grace.

Ack, that the Word would become drudgery! Almost so much that it dulls the sweet reality behind it. Young priests often go out in service with something of a vision for the future. The years go by, and one or another might be realized. Most simply aren't. And so comes resignation—completely unwarranted! It happens now after so many disappointments: Behold, now is the time of joy. Behold, now is the day of salvation! It happens yet in the evening of life when one has run out of his best energy. It is really not the end of His mercifulness. It is just as effective and real now as when I went out with fresh energy and burning eagerness realizing what I placed in my prayers and my hope. Now, because even a *seelsorger* has a merciful Savior, who is not finished forgiving, one may always begin again with the same good mood, as a laymen may begin each and every new day though she never becomes perfect and can never quit praying for forgiveness. It is so also with our work in the Church and in the parish. It is just as imperfect and is always full of shortcomings. And yet we can do it with joy, because grace and forgiveness overshadow it, because the Word of absolution is perpetually ringing over it anew. So long as the voice sounds from heaven, so long as a new day of grace dawns, it is an enjoyable time with all God's possibilities hiding in morning's bosom.

And so we can end with a word from the Early Church's greatest *seelsorger*: "Therefore, my beloved brothers, be steadfast, immovable, always abounding in the work of the Lord, knowing that in the Lord your labor is not in vain" (1 Cor. 15:58 ESV).

The kernel of wheat must die. What has been said from the pulpit today?

BELIEF AND FALSE-BELIEF

Presented at Church Day in Växjo and Eksjö in 1961

The word *false-belief* is an unusual word in our language. Maybe because the issue is being lost. For many men all faith is approximately the same. It happens that one has a quite particular concept of faith, a modern dogma about faith. The dogma isn't always formulated clearly. Often, he is hardly conscious of it. But it is there and exercises its power over people.

This dogma says that people cannot know anything particular about God. We may have our own thoughts and feelings, some have a religious disposition, and some also have strong religious moods, but altogether these are our highest personal experiences and interpretations of a reality that is much harder to access. Therefore, all faith is subjective. Therefore, all faith that rests on a serious conviction must also be seen as just as good. Therefore, it is arrogant and abusive to talk about false-belief. Who dares to state that another man's thoughts and beliefs about God are false?

One would be able to agree with all this and it would in large part be right, if there were not a great "but." This "but" is Jesus Christ.

That no man has ever seen God, this too is a Christian belief. But just where that is written, there follows the important addition: "the only begotten Son, who Himself is God, who is at the Father's side, He has made Him known."

This is not some little meaningless addition to the Christian faith. It belongs to the heart of the matter. We believe in a God who wants "all men to be saved and come to the knowledge of truth" (1 Tim. 2:4) and who, for just that reason, has sent His Son into the world and made it possible for us to come to the knowledge of the truth, to know God, to know His will, and to know the way that leads to Him.

To say, "I believe in Jesus Christ," also means to say, "I believe that one can know God. I believe that God has revealed Himself. I believe that the true light who gives light to every man, He has come into the world," as John says.

It is just this that the apostles constantly repeat: We saw His glory. The life, the eternal that was from the Father, it has been revealed, and we have seen it. Before Christ, the world lived in times of ignorance. In such times of ignorance, God was patient. But now He invites men everywhere that they should repent. Now the ignorance is no longer excused.

And no one has said this clearer than Jesus Himself: "No one knows the Father, but the Son, and he for whom the Son will make Him known." "No one has seen the Father, but He who is from the Father. He has seen the Father." "No one comes to the Father, but through Me." If one does not dismiss Jesus as an enthusiast or swindler, then one must take this seriously. And if one takes this seriously, then one may reconsider all his modern dogmas about faith and test them before Jesus Christ. Let him test them and see if they hold.

So what is faith?

Is it only our thoughts and our groping experiences of the God of whom we still cannot conceive?

The Scriptures answer that it can be. Overwhelmingly much of the religious faith that is found on earth also in our day and age and in our land is precisely of this type. For the Scriptures say, God has created "every nation of mankind [so] that they should seek God in the hope that they might feel their way toward him" (Acts 17:26-27). He has written His Law on their hearts, so that even the heathen have at least some concept of what is right and wrong. He has even revealed His invisible being in creation, His eternal power and divine glory in creation, so that one can conceive of Him from His work.

Also there really is a common knowledge of God, in all people and in all times. But it is a seeking concept that grabs after a shadow, a reflex that is never able to conceive. It is a groping that often grabs the wrong thing, and a seeking that encounters many false paths or goes astray in the dark because there are so many contrary voices, so many incoherent contradictions, and so many completely man-made religions in the world.

If we now come before Christ with all this, we get the simple answer, "I am the light of the world. He who follows me will not walk in the darkness, but will have the light of life" (John 8:12).

This answer would be pure arrogance if He were not who He says He is. Before this answer, many can say with the Pharisees: "You are bearing witness about Yourself; Your testimony is not true." With this answer one has joined the Pharisees and put himself on the side of those who reject Jesus. And finally there are only two possibilities here: either Jesus is right or He is wrong. Either one says with Peter, "You are the Messiah, the living son of God," or one says like Caiaphas, "He has uttered blasphemy. What further witness do we need?"

We Christians believe that Christ was right. His teaching was from God and not from man. It was not insanity, bragging or arrogance when He spoke about the Father who had sent Him. He was sent from God, who lives in a light where no one can come. He knows Him. He came to make Him known. And therefore He is the way, the truth, and the life.

Therefore, it is also a faith that is more than our human thoughts. There is a faith that separates itself from human religious notions like clear, exact, and well-grounded knowledge separates itself from amateurish speculations. The Christian meaning of faith is namely not a supposition or thought about something that one really can't know, but it is a knowledge, it is a knowing of the reality that is otherwise hidden from us. And God Himself has given us this knowledge, He who desires that we shall come to knowledge of the truth.

That faith is something other than a thought. One knew that already in Israel. In the preparation that God has done, when He gave His people the promise and the Law, he had also given His people an insight into faith's existence that goes far beyond what many people think today. It is expressed already in the Old Testament's word for faith. This word is really from the same stem as the word truth. Truth (emeth) in the Old Testament means first and foremost God's truth that is a possession of God that can be described most closely as faithfulness. It is something that belongs to God's essence and His divine glory. Therefore, grace belongs to His noblest gifts. All His commands are truth, and His Law is truth. God's truth is all His faithful intentions and desires for life and man. It is the righteousness and peace that He in His faithfulness creates and sustains when men enter into His covenant. And to believe is to assent to this truth, to see that God is faithful, to answer His faithfulness with faith and reliance, love and obedience. This characteristic is seen in that the word faith (heemin) comes from the same stem as the words truth and faithfulness. It is also a verb that answers to substantive meaning. Such a verb we do not have in Swedish. One would be able to attempt to render this word with "assent" and "make true," since one exercises the truth when one believes. One takes it up in himself, lets it work on him, is carried by it, lives by it, and follows it.

It also means to believe in biblical meaning. It does not mean to make subjective and uncertain thoughts for oneself about God. It is to meet God's reality, grab hold of it, know it, and live according to it.

The way in which the New Testament views truth and speaks of it is noticeable enough to anyone who reads the Bible. The truth is not just a piece of knowledge. No, the truth is a piece of God. It gives expression to His will, His meaning, and the right order in life. Therefore, it speaks about doing the truth, to stand in the truth, to be of truth. The opposite is Satan's being. He is the father of lies, and he does not stand in the truth. But Christ is the truth. He not only knows it, but he is the truth. And to believe in him means just to see this truth, to assent to it, be filled by it, and live according to it.

Therefore, it also means separating belief from false-belief. Yes, it is important to do this. To posit that all faith can be just as right, or to say that all human faith is only a human thought concerning God, that is to reject Christ. It is to say that God has not revealed Himself as He has done. It is to push away from oneself God's truth, who has been sent to us.

We must also separate faith that gropes after the truth that God has revealed in Christ and false-belief that builds upon human attempts to search for God.

False-belief can certainly have even a large fragment of a true knowledge of God, but it is still a false-belief if it denies the essential truth that God gave us in Christ. Even the Pharisees in their faith had large pieces of the right knowledge of God, more than most of the other men of the time. But they rejected the truth.

There is a religiosity in our land that conceives of itself as Christian without desiring to be churchly. It has a place for prayer, even if the prayer is not regular. It has a place for sporadic visiting of the church, not for a regular and active engagement in the congregation's life. And the Lord's Supper tends to fall completely outside its scope, except in isolated, rare, and exceptional cases.

This confession of faith is something like the following: I believe that there is a God. He is good, and desires that we shall be good. After death there is eternal life.

What should we say about such a faith?

It is apparent that it contains pieces of the truth. These pieces come partly out of the universal revelation in nature and consciousness, but partly out of the Scriptures and from Christ.

That God exists, that He is worth praying to and is praised, that He demands us to live rightly, the heathen know that. It is written in creation and in the hearts of men. Certainty that God is good comes from the Gospel. It belongs with that which Christ revealed, when He taught us to know the heavenly Father, who lets the sun shine on the evil as well as the good.

But what place does Christ have in this faith?

Usually there is also a place for Him there as the great teacher and example. He has given us wise and good rules for life and a shining example that we should imitate. He has assured us that God is good and that there really is life after death.

And, of course, all this is true!

But it is not the complete truth. It is a truth with such great gaps that it no longer tells us the truth of salvation and the way to God.

What is missing?

"The most important," one could answer—everything our fathers meant when they spoke about the basis of salvation, means, and order. Here is missing the very basic evangelical truths, those that Luther struggled with in the monastery.

Even more, it is missing the means of grace. Baptism has ceased to have any meaning for the Christian life. The Word is no longer the bread of life, what one really needs to keep his soul alive. And the Lord's Supper is almost completely forgotten right after one goes forward to his first Communion. And all this one neglects without having any concept that these means of grace are the only means through which one can receive God's grace. He is lacking also blessed order and the truth that God will carry out something through His Word that will lead us to repentance and new faith that God day by day creates in us through His Word.

Here also are lacking the very truths that Luther rediscovered, and which are the cornerstones of Christendom. One no longer knows to be justified by faith in Jesus. Instead one has a vague and blurred faith in works as the way to God. It is our nature to believe that if we do right then we must please God. The conscience tells us that God wills that we shall do right. God's own Law tells us the same. One may believe that if one lives even a tolerably respectable life and endeavors to not do anything wrong, then it must go well in the end. If one believes this, one has lost the truth that the New Testament inculcates more than any other: that no deed can make us righteous before God, because we always come short before the two most important commandments. We are to love God above all things and our neighbor as ourselves, and, therefore, only faith in Jesus can give us the righteousness that stands before God, that which Jesus won for us through His obedience and His death.

Also lost is the truth about the Word that was the Reformation's other discovery. Luther never tired of inculcating that it is only through His Word that God deals with us. Through the Word, we receive all our knowledge about Him and salvation, but not only knowledge but also the heart's right relationship. Through the Word, God awakens repentance in our heart; through the Word, He creates faith. Through the Word, He keeps it with His power. Therefore, no one can be a Christian without the Word and the work that it carries out for us when we use it regularly.

The faith that lacks all this must be called false-belief. And then it is false-belief only so long as we think it is enough, so that it hinders and keeps us away from Christ, His Church, and His salvation. It is false-belief if it leads us to be satisfied with a Christ who is only an example, for an example is only a piece of law, not Gospel. This law condemns us like all other laws.

Two things are needed for Christian faith: that the Word is rightly proclaimed and that men take care to hear it. There is needed a right proclamation that clearly and intelligibly speaks about who Christ is and what He has done for us. Perhaps, the proclamation's most dangerous temptation in this time is to cautiously adapt itself, so that his proclamation will tolerably fit with the patterns of thought that are the usual among religiously minded people. It need not mean that he says something completely wrong. But the proclamation is cautious and unclear. It avoids speaking directly to the matter and so unites with common religiosity's way of seeing things. But then there is no clear reply about the basis of salvation, means, and order. Therefore, the proclaimer must instruct and speak about who Jesus is with all the power and fervency he is able to muster, so that no one can escape noticing how the Church's whole message is penetrated by the apostolic word: "Believe in Jesus, and you will be saved."

But just as important is the other need: that men come and hear the proclamation. Every Christian ought to be conscious about the particular responsibility he has at just this time, so that men again shall understand that going to church to hear and use God's Word is not a dispensable and indifferent matter, but that it is the first vital condition for all of Christendom.

Much of the violent debate that rose in the Church concerning the Lord's Supper, marriage, faithfulness to Scripture, and much else came about because men suddenly realized that Christianity is not at all about the common religiosity and idealism as they thought. It has been a shocking discovery for them that the Church, in all seriousness, stands for a revelation, a truth about God that God Himself has given us. But that shock is a healthy sign. The Church would be dead and would never serve her Lord if she only had something else to say about the common religiosity that omitted the only Savior and His eternally applicable Word.

Therefore, we shall rejoice about the storms. It would be better if they didn't have to come. But we shall pray that the unrest may be an awakening unrest that causes men to begin to listen to their own words. And we must consider our own responsibility. That although we walk in the flesh so we struggle against the flesh as Paul says. Though we live here in the flesh as pardoned sinners who together are sinners and yet are God's children, we must therefore discipline our old Adam so that he is not the one fighting. It is not us and our glory we fight for. It is for the salvation of men, first and foremost those who now do not know what the Christian faith is. We may not give them the impression that the fight is only about human meaning, and to each his own. One gets this impression if we fight according to the flesh as if fighting for prestige, with bitterness and unworthy polemics. The fight for souls is not to be carried out in this manner. That which best shows that this is God's thing and God's Word is a holy life and a chivalrous fight that show that one stands under God's Word Himself, and that the Word has power over one's own heart.

LOVE YOUR BROTHER

Pastoral Conference, 1962

It ought to be easy for a pastor to speak to the office about "loving his brother." I believe that most of my brothers in the office understand me when I say that it is one of the hardest things a man can do.

Theoretically, it is not so hard to report what the Scriptures teach us about love. God is love, and the love comes from God. He who does not love has not learned to love God. But he who loves is born of God. This belongs with rebirth: we share in God's love. When we are justified through faith and have peace with God through our Lord Jesus Christ, then God's love is poured out in our hearts through the Holy Spirit (Rom. 5). And this love compels us. It cannot be ineffective.

It is also logical that this is called a new commandment. For God's love has been revealed among us in Christ, because God sent His only begotten Son as an atonement for our sins. Only he who has the Son can love with His love. Only he can understand what this love is about, for this is love: "Not that we have loved God [with our religious longing, our seeking, our attempts to obey the conscience, or what we men can bring about before Christ and without Christ] but this is love, that He has loved us and sent us His Son." Therefore Jesus can say to the Jews, "I know you and know that you do not bear God's love in your heart." Yet to the Thessalonians, Paul can write, "You yourselves have been taught by God to love one another" (1 Thess. 4:9).

So it is also. Therefore, it ought to be the love that stamps all of our Christian lives, that which separates us from the normal life in the world. When it comes to pastors, this ought to be our characteristic, and in our relationships with one another it ought to be a self-evident thing, just as self-evident as the saltiness of salt and the shining of a light. "You are the salt of the earth." "You are the light of the world. Can a city that sits on a hill be hidden?"

But is it so? A pastor asks the question of his own heart. He can judge according to the results of a daily repentance for many years. Is it so?

The love that comes from God and that lives in all of those who are born of God, it should also show itself in relationships with my brothers. "He who does not love his brother whom he has seen, he cannot love God whom he has not seen."

My brother, whom I have seen . . . Just he who I have seen in close proximity, in the daily wear and tear of working together. Perhaps, I have seen his mistakes and even suffered for them. For it happens that my brother is forgetful and negligent. He dodges his most troublesome tasks, and so it becomes my task instead (or I become the scapegoat for it not being done). Or it happens that my brother has another view of the word, he will have it done in a different way. Perhaps we have discussed the matter, and it is completely frustrating because we think completely different. Maybe I have a feeling that he criticizes me. I suspect that he is filled with *schadenfreude* when I fail with my way of working. He sees well that he has approval of the parishioners for his way of doing the work for the congregation. Maybe I have a feeling that he spreads polemics against me in the pulpit or writing. And time and time again I come to this, that I do not love him—my brother whom I have seen.

Maybe I excuse myself by thinking he really isn't my brother (in the biblical meaning). For my brother is he who is my brother in the Lord, in the same faith in Christ, in the purity and fullness of it. Maybe I have begun to question whether one or another brother in the office really is my brother in the Lord, if there must not be something wrong with his relationship to the Lord Himself. And is it not rightly placed there when he belongs to them who stand outside and between me and him there is an abyss that goes so deep that it separates us for all eternity.

But if this were so, is this any excuse? It is true that there is a difference between the brotherly love and the common. But I should as a Christian also possess the common love. And this reaches to all God's created children, also to those who come across as being my enemies or persecutors, even to those who hate me and laughingly say all evil against me. For God's sun rises up over both the evil and good, and I would be my heavenly Father's child also in this way: that I really loved as Him and not only my brothers. It is this common love that Peter calls agape—the brotherly is called philadelphia—and agape is just this love of God that shall be found in my heart if I belong to God. It all depends on whether I have faith that is effective through this agape, this love that even loves his enemies.

I don't want to escape. I should not, of course, love my neighbor and hate my enemies. I should love him. But how is it possible?

When I have gone with this embarrassed and guilty conscience to ask my New Testament, so I soon discovered that this love was not there either, not there among the Christians. It was not a self-evident thing. It was self-evident that it should be there. But it was not self-evident that it was. If such were the case, the apostles would not have needed to constantly remind and admonish the Christians to love, as they in fact did.

Christ Himself says to His apostles, "Remain in My love." And here is an if: "If you (keep My commandments), you remain in My love, if you love one another." And Paul's admonishment: "Love one another with brotherly affection." "Let love be genuine." "But the greatest of these is love." And Peter says, "Above all keep loving one another earnestly." And all that John wrote can be summed up in the end with the penetrating exhortation: "Love one another."

The contrary is also found there, apparently as a bitter experience, even among those who had been counted as God's chosen: "You shall love your neighbor as yourself, but if you bite and devour one another, watch that you are not consumed by one another." One can determine to walk in love. One can tell himself to love God but hate his brother.

It is also apparent that love never has been a self-evident and easy application, something that one possessed without fighting and without risk of losing it. How should he be able to do it? It is of course God's love that is revealed in His only begotten Son, in Him who has been given for us. We possess it only when we have the Son. Just as one can separate himself from forgiveness in Christ, so can one separate the love from him. Therefore He says, "Remain in My love," just as He says, "Remain in Me." He means to walk in the love just the same as we walk in the Lord or in the Spirit. It says to clothe yourself in love in the same way that it speaks of clothing yourself with Christ.

But we only have Christ in faith. If anyone is Christ's, then he is a new creation. Something new has happened, the old is past. The old is the Law's judgment, the time of wrath, the bondage under the strong man, who watches over his house and his possessions. It is past, but the flesh is not past. The Law that is in our members always attempts to assert its influence. The world, the fallen, remains with all of its temptations. Therefore the Spirit and the flesh must now be in conflict with one another. And all that I possess in Christ, I possess certainly, completely, and fully before God, so that I am His child, but here in the daily reality I possess it only while I fight for it, only partially and only to the extent that Christ lives in me.

This is also true of love. It is the same as Christ in me. When I received Christ and His forgiveness in daily repentance, then His love also comes to me, God's love. It is therefore as Christ says, he who receives only a little forgiveness, so he also loves little.

And now I have gotten to the right departure point in order to be able to conceive, and realize, something about loving my brother. Here is first the comfort that I so well need. It is not hopeless for me, though I so often come short. I can still be a child of God. But this comfort is no rest cushion for my old Adam. It is really awful that I fall short. When we do not love one another, then the consequences come, as Jesus says, that men cannot understand that we are His disciples. It can be one of the main reasons that they do not bother to hear us. The Spirit's fruit is love, it is written, first and foremost, love. And it is the Spirit's fruit that men have the right to expect of us. According to the fruit, one shall judge the tree, and it is the fruit that exposes false prophets. It is also really very bad if I do not bear the fruit that belongs to repentance.

But again there is a comfort. When the Bible so obviously admonishes to love, then there is in this a promise that it really is something that we can do. It only means to command that which I can do and show how I can do it.

Let us begin by looking at a well-known verse of Peter's: "Having purified your souls by your obedience to the truth for a sincere brotherly love, love one another earnestly from a pure heart" (1 Pet. 1:22 ESV).

It is really written, "Since you have purified your souls [hēgnikótes = through a sanctifying act)], so that you now are pure." And this has happened "in obedience to the truth." The context very clearly says what this concerns. Just before it had described how we have been ransomed, not with gold or silver, but with the precious blood of Christ. Through faith we now have access to God, because, as it is written, this faith is also "a hope in God." In this faith also happens the purification in obedience to the truth. The truth is as always the divine truth, God's good meaning for life, His plan for our redemption. The obedience to the truth means to recognize our sin—otherwise, we make God a liar, as John says—and to believe in Christ, who is our only, but also sufficient, hope.

This is also the departure point, and it is very important. To this departure point, we must continually return. And it is this that can be so hard, not the least for a wretched pastor, who is overburdened with work and has to toil to prepare his next sermon amidst visitation, telephone conversations, paperwork, mediations, church administration, and confirmation instruction. In the morning his telephone or the doorbell already rings, and in the evening one is dead tired. It is so easy that his own devotion and prayers become pushed aside, there is not peace for self-examination—one must, of course, keep it all going. So one becomes spiritually self-supporting; one figures that he is in essence right with himself. The greater problem comes from this. One addresses them with the same energy, but that means that this energy begins to flow from human wells, one's own energy, one's own wisdom and experience, but not out of the love of the Lord Christ who has His well in the forgiveness of sins that I must every day anew avail myself to that which makes my heart humble, thankful, willing to obey, and able to love for His sake.

I must also sanctify and purify my heart in obedience to this truth that I so well know but which I shall also practice. Only then can I continue with the apostles, "Having purified your souls by your obedience to the truth for a sincere brotherly love." It is also this that according to Paul is the result, as the purification in Christ's blood leads to: sincere brotherly love (philadelphia). When I receive it in this act of purification that means faith in the forgiveness of my sins for Christ sake, then love becomes sincere (anypokritos). And only then. The love that is born of my human energy and my duty of conscience, it is forced, self-assumed work of the Law. But when Christ's love is really in my heart, Christ's love for me, which is the same as He Himself being in my heart, then there is also unfeigned love for the brothers.

And to all this now belongs this perfect tense that the admonition begins with. When all this has happened and is there as a completed fact, then comes the admonition: love one another earnestly from a pure heart. And just to show what the basis is, Peter continues, "Since you have been born again, not of perishable seed but of imperishable, through the living and abiding word of God" (1 Pet. 1:23 ESV). It is this which is born anew through the Word that kills and makes alive, buries and raises, which can love with the heart and with sustainable love. We notice how Peter says the same about John: "He who loves is born of God."

What I here can and may do is to come to my Lord Christ and pray for this miracle. Pray for forgiveness for all, pray for His own presence, pray that He will live in me, so that I no longer live for myself, pray that His love for me makes it so I can say, "Lord, You know all, You know that I love You," and that means that I love His will, His kingdom, His coming, as Paul says in his old age.

But then I also have this concretely: to love my brother. We have already said that it is a comfort that so many obvious admonitions to love occur. This is Christ's command, "Love one another." Here there must also be something that I can and ought to do. It is with love as with everything else. God is He who works both the will and the act. Still I shall myself work with fear and trembling. Therefore this admonition to love remains first among all the other admonitions. I shall not only expect that this will be given to me; I shall pray for it. I shall know where the only well is. But at the same time, I will hold fast to this which God puts on me in my daily desires and my daily course. And there it belongs too that I shall love my brother.

Let us take an example. In 1 Corinthians 16, Paul says, "Let all you do be done in love." It is the crown in a council of other admonishments: "Be watchful, stand firm in the faith, act like men, be strong." Now I know that I cannot do this either if Christ does not do it for me, in me, through me. Shall I be watchful of my own power? Then it will go as it did in Gethsemane. How can I stand firm in the faith if God does not create the faith constantly anew within my heart? How can I be a man and be strong when I am by nature scared, shy, and insecure before men? And then these are real admonitions. There is something that I shall and can do in faith. I can be watchful by giving attention to the Word, and in my heart, instead of being careless with my devotion or reading the Bible only with thought to my preaching and what I shall say to others. I can stand fast when the tempter tries to make me buckle under and compromise in questions of good confession. I can be a man and be strong when I am confronted with the choice between saying that which is harmless and half true and saying what I know the text means. In the same manner, I stand again and again before the hard decision of loving my brother.

Here it really isn't in the first place a matter of feelings, nor is it about being able to say friendly things. It is not about loving in word and with the tongue, but in deed and truth. When it says in Romans 12, "Love one another with brotherly affection," so continues Paul immediately, "Outdo one another in showing honor. Do not be slothful in zeal, be fervent in spirit, serve the Lord. Rejoice in hope, be patient in tribulation, be constant in prayer. Contribute to the needs of the saints and seek to show hospitality" (vv. 10–13 ESV). When I ask how I shall be able to love my brother, then God answers that I at least can do Him some little service. The question is not in the first place what I can be able to feel for him but what I do for him if I have eyes for his worries and difficulties and am willing to take upon myself a piece of his burden. And it is remarkable that many men, who really don't have a charming personality and really don't have an immediate winsome manner, still for others become their best friends and are able to convince skeptics that Christ is real by doing real service where it is really needed. So should any of us in the society be able to go a second mile for a tolerably pressing and self-interested fellow creature. So ought we not vex ourselves about it. It is, of course, just in this manner that the kingdom of heaven shows itself here on earth, Jesus says.

Therefore, it is not love to blur out the line between truth and lies in the spiritual. If it is our own truth, we can give it up for the sake of love, but not Christ's truth. There is false teaching. It causes division and opens wounds in Christ's Church. Such cannot be healed by compromising where one lets anything go in questions of faith. The brotherly love, that which binds together those who are members in the same Lord Christ, cannot unite those who are not brothers in the faith. But even here the common love applies. False teaching is sin, and one shall hate all sin. But one shall love the sinner. It belongs to this love that one does not distort what he says, does not accuse him for that which he has not said or for that which he has not done. Belonging to this love means that one tries to understand and conceive rightly and that one cautiously tests if it is possibly still God's truth that he believes in and lives by, even if the formulas are defective or maybe just unfamiliar to me.

In the hard situation in our church, which we all suffer, it is not the way to unity to only say that we shall love one another. Each and every one of us knows that love does not mean for us to become one with Baptists, still less with the Jehovah's Witnesses. There are contradictions in the teaching that go so deep that we cannot bridge them with love. For Christ's love is something more than human ability to draw together. It is the loving communion with Christ, who needs the pure Gospel to remain.

It is not possible for love's sake to do that which one is certain that Christ forbade and that Christ dislikes. It is that which makes the division in our church so serious. When such happens that is to some a waste, the consequence is that some turn their back on the church. It can mean that they go to Rome. We know that it contains something shockingly serious, something that can mean that the party concerned is lost, him, my brother, who Christ suffered and died for. Precisely the same problem is found in the early congregations. Paul did not hesitate about how one should handle them. Such should not happen; one shouldn't take the risk. If one still has cause for it to happen, then one no longer walks in the love, or he waves his use of freedom that he certainly possessed in Christ. So it would be good if those who think they have the freedom to ordain women to the pastoral office refrain from using the freedom rather than let it cause offense and stumbling.

I know that the matter seems different from their point of view. It is that which is so serious and hard that we have come to this point where we see the Word with such different points of view, that we have come to conflicting and incompatible practices. When this happens it is only reasonable that one of the systems is false.

In any case, for he who will see the matter from the Gospel's own point of view, there cannot be any doubt about what He commands here: You shall love. All that we know of the love of God, who gave Himself for us to be able to live in us sinners, it ought here show its reality. I have already said that it does not mean compromise. But it ought to mean a love for our conceptual opponents, who do not hold a grudge for the sake of injury that does not rejoice over unrighteousness and who, therefore, disdain all unrighteous arguments and all false reproach. This love has its joy in the truth. It rejoices also when it can find a piece of truth in a conceptual opponent. It believes everything, and it hopes all things when it comes to possibilities to love from the truth even for he who does not see it.

This love is not a cheap way to atonement blurring the lines of truth. But in a deeper sense, it is the only possible way to atonement. Where this love is not found by them who will stand for the truth, there they no longer stand for truth. For Christ's truth cannot be where Christ's love is not, love also for the sinner. But where Christ's love is, there can also be the cure that heals deficiencies in our knowledge and our prophesying.

So I stand again before the serious question: do I have love? Or am I possibly only a thundering cloud and a clamoring cymbal? And again I turn back to the only foundation that keeps, to Him who has loved me and given His life for me, and here I finally have the only guarantee and the only comfort. If I hold fast to Him, then nothing can take me away, nothing that man, the world, Satan, or death can threaten me with. No, in all this I shall win a glorious victory through Him who has loved me. And I may be certain that neither death nor life shall be able to separate me from God's love in Christ Jesus my Lord.

THE CHURCH'S WAY TODAY

Oslo, 1962

What is the Church's way today?

What is meant by "the Church's way"?

It may mean approximately the same thing as when one speaks about the Church's program or the Church's work methods, her goal-setting and the means with which she will attain her objectives—just like an association, a party, or some other societal organization.

But this only skims the surface of the problem. The Church's way is something more and something deeper.

One discovers it if one goes to the New Testament and sees that the Church is quite simply called "the Way." It happens in many verses in Acts. In our Swedish translation, it is written "this way," but in the original text, it is written simply "the Way." It says that Saul went to the High Priest and secured his recommendation to the Jews in Damascus to be able to arrest those who might belong to "the Way." It says that the Jews in Ephesus spoke ill of "the Way," and that later in the city there was a lot of unrest concerning "the Way." It is written of Governor Felix that he knew "the Way" very well—carrying this meaning: Christendom, the congregation, the Church. And Paul says in his speech before Felix, "But this I confess to you, that according to the Way, which they call a sect, I worship the God of our fathers" (Acts 24:14 ESV).

This last bit is very revealing. The Christians also call themselves "the Way," while the Jews call it a *hairesis*. This is the same word that we have in heresy, the word for false doctrine and sect.

The word did not mean the same thing at that time. It meant choice or decision in classical Greek. It can also mean that which one makes a decision for or selects, for example a standpoint or a philosophical opinion. So for example, the Stoic school of philosophy or Platonists could be called heresies. The same meaning is used at the same time for the movements within Judaism, for example, the Pharisees or the Sadducees. But here, with Paul, it has a small hint of condescension. The others call us a *hairesis* he says, but we are "the Way." This difference is essential for early Christendom and for all Christendom.

A *hairesis* is a movement, a faction, a party with its program. It is something that one chooses, implying one among many other thoughtful opinions. But Christendom is something more. It is not one opinion among other opinions, not just one way of thinking, not just a manifestation of the zeitgeist. But it knows of itself that it builds upon an intervention of God that happened once and for all, in a manner that has consequences for every age. This claim is clearly expressed behind the whole person and work of Jesus. There lies in His own word "I am the Way." He explains what this means in the same context: "No one comes to the Father but through Me." He is the one who has come to seek and save those who are lost. He is the only-begotten Son. Whoever believes in Him shall be saved. Once and for all, He has sacrificed Himself. Peter expresses it pregnantly and classically when he says before the great council: "And there is salvation in no one else, for there is no other name under heaven given among men by which we must be saved" (Acts 4:12 ESV).

Therefore, Christendom is something more than an opinion, one truth among others. Therefore, early Christendom defended itself from being called a *hairesis*. It is the Way. God's way, the way of truth, the way of salvation, the way of righteousness, and however else one might say it. It is quite simply the Way, the way opened by God, that which the Son paved with His death, the way that passes through forgiveness, the way of reconciliation and forgiveness through faith in Jesus, the only one who leads to the Father. It is at the same time the narrow way, and they are few who find it and walk upon it. It is not a manifestation of the zeitgeist, not something that answers to the zeitgeist and popular opinion. Jesus calls us to go this way when He says with all His authority, "Follow Me," and one may for the most part go against the current.

In a newly published work, "Church Fathers, Heretics and Councils," Helmut Echternach has emphasized this. And he makes the reflection that this has been the reason that heretics and heresies of all ages have been popular. Heretics say that which is in the air, that which men think, that which strikes them as self-evident on grounds of particular time-bound conclusions that lie underneath every age and science, and these thoughts give the impression of being free and unbound. In these cases, the Early Church was right to use the word heresy. Here it is a matter of one's opinion, one current of thought, one of many that have been lost to others in the course of time, and which in every age become the party line and is used in orientation. But Christendom, the Gospel, the Church is the Way, because Christ is the way, the only way that leads to God.

The Church's way is also in the deepest sense Christ. The Church is, according to Jesus' own words, built upon Peter's confession, "You are the Messiah, the living God's Son." Only so long as she stands on the rock is she His Church. But so long as she stands there she is so radically different than just an opinion, a direction, a heresy. She is the Way.

Now if we ask, what is the Church's way today, then we must answer that the Church today must be the way in the same manner as in the apostles' time and in every age. It means that she must immovably hold fast to (as Jude says) the faith, which has been once and for all delivered to the saints. Here God has intervened in the world. Here something has happened that neither can nor needs to be redone or built upon. It stands there, once for all delivered. God's Son has come into the world, died, and rose again. If the Church is to be the Church, then she must be immovably faithful to her Christ. This means that she is also faithful to the apostolic message and to the Word, such as it is given in the Holy Scriptures. For it belongs to our faith in God's intervention in the world through Christ that this Christ sent His apostles and gave them His Holy Spirit, the Spirit of truth, who would also lead them into all truth. They have not corrupted the message nor made Jesus into something other than He was. But they have spoken "by the Holy Spirit sent from heaven," as they say. Their message belongs to God's intervention in the world. The whole Bible belongs to it. It is just this that characterizes Jesus' own view of the Bible. It is obvious for Him that it is God's Word. He refers men to the Bible's word with their questions about God's will and God's way. With the word of the Bible, he rejects the tempter. With the word of the Bible, he refutes both Pharisees and Sadducees when they come with their false assertions and their insidious questions.

I shall not here go into all that of which such a faith consists. I only demonstrate that it has belonged to Christendom from the beginning. "How from childhood you have been acquainted with the sacred writings, which are able to make you wise for salvation through faith in Christ Jesus" (2 Tim. 3:15 ESV).

The Church's way is also that which even at its very beginning was called "the Way." The Church has had its way staked out and may not stray from it. The Church is the message about what God has done in history, something that cannot be undone and cannot be made something else. The Gospel proclaims these facts and bids people to believe in them. These facts are active in the Church. They step constantly anew in history. Christ is risen. He speaks His Word. He meets us people so that we can hear that it is He who speaks. He forgives sins and makes us know that we are forgiven. The Word is not only a deed that tells what once happened. The Word is a means of grace, the means God has chosen through which to come to us with His grace. The Sacraments are not only symbols. They are God's means, deeds that He carries out before our eyes. Christ makes us into His disciples in Baptism. He dines with us in the Lord's Supper. Through these means He comes to us and gives Himself to us.

The Church's way is therefore the same in every age: to rightly proclaim the Word and properly administer the Sacraments as Christ commanded. Where this happens, there is "the Way," that which leads to God. Therefore, our Confessions also say that this true Church is found wherever the Word is rightly proclaimed and the Sacraments rightly administered.

Here steadfastness and firmness are always needed. That which sounds so easy is the great test of faith for the Church in every generation. Of course, we live in a world that is constantly changing. When it comes to technology, medicine, and law-making there is a constant development.

This development belongs to God's work in creation. God has given mankind her reason and placed her above all nature. She can and should create better conditions for herself on the earth. But there is one thing that God has excepted from the law of development. The Gospel and the whole of God's work of salvation is given in a form that is definitive. All this that God revealed about Himself and His plans for the world—something that we otherwise would never have been able to know—that we cannot improve upon. We have been given to know what we need to know, and it is given to us in a form that we cannot change.

It belongs to our human hubris that we gladly seek to turn this upside down. We would gladly rule over revelation too and control knowledge about God. We want to determine what is reasonable and acceptable even when it comes to God. The consequence can only be that one completely rejects the idea of God, declaring that it is illogical and unreasonable. But it can also lead one to become deeply religious, yet still rejecting God's revelation in Christ and the Word. One accepts only the knowledge of God one can get from her own conscience and her own experience. Of course, people have been given a sense of God's glory in nature. She, at least, encounters a glimpse of his holy will in her conscience. So long as she can interpret this herself, she might accept it. She might complement this with the best she has found in poetry and philosophy. That which seems plausible or relatively self evident is, of course, that which lies in line with the time's popular views and with all the unclear, but powerful conclusions behind what is called the zeitgeist.

This religiosity is Christendom's greatest enemy. Not all religiosity, but that which will form the Gospel according to the thinking of the time and according to its own valuations. There is a religiosity that is the preliminary stage to the Christian faith. About this Jesus says that it comes to the light. It is found among those who are of the truth and seek truth. They are drawn instinctively to the truth, even when they meet God in the heart and in the wonders of creation, and when they meet the Gospel, the true light, they come to Christ "so that it will be made clear that His deeds have been carried out in God."

But such is not all religiosity. There is a piety that will not leave the reigns or will in any case not lose hold of its right to be able to determine for itself what kind of God is reasonable. It has an instinctive opposition to the revelation of God in the Word, against the God who comes to us in the means of grace, presented by His Church.

Few of the Church's fathers have seen this as clearly as Luther saw this, or fought it as powerfully as he fought it. He calls these prophets of common religiosity schwarmerei.[1] He does not hesitate to point to their great cardinal mistake: that they put their own heart's thoughts and feelings and their immoderate revelations against the true revelation in Christ and the Word. They want to find God everywhere but where He really allows Himself to be found: in the means of grace. They adduce the Spirit's leading and the Spirit's illumination, but they do not understand that the Spirit and the Word belong inseparably together.

They have never understood why we, in the Third Article, confess both the Holy Spirit and the one Holy Christian Church in the same breath.

It is not modern to speak of schwarmerei. But the matter is modern to a high degree. The beloved heresy of our day lies completely and clearly along this line. Certainly there is a deep-seated difference here. In Luther's day the schwarmerei, the enthusiasts, acknowledged that

---

[1] Schwarmerei is a term Luther used for enthusiasts, the picture is of bees swarming a beehive with mass confusion and busyness.

Jesus was Christ, God's Son. It was only this, that one sought to know His will through one's own revelations and played them over and against the Bible's revelation that one interpreted according to his own principles. Our day's schwarmerei usually have a different Christology. They believe in God and they believe in the morals, that God must be good and merciful, a heavenly Father who loves us all and finally gathers us in His arms. And Jesus? He has shown us that this is God's temperament. He has given us an incomparable foreshadowing of this life as the loving God's will that we shall live. But the New Testament's Christ does not fit well in this system. God's Son who bears our sin and atones for them, the Savior who is the only way to the Father, is fundamentally unnecessary—as is salvation through faith in Jesus. Such redemption has never been needed, Christ never wanted to be worshiped, faith in His ethical norms and obedience to them are more important than faith in Christ Himself. Here, nothing more is needed than repentance and moral improvement. Here is needed no Baptism, no Lord's Supper, no regular use of the Word. There is no need to be united with the Savior through daily repentance and faith and to take part in His righteousness. The most essential in this religiosity can be found in the universal revelation. From this illumination one can gather together the essentials of Christendom in the words God, virtue, and immortality. The essentials become belief in God, do the right thing, and acknowledge the soul's immortality. One looks undogmatic but in reality has some very particular dogmas. To them belong faith in development and the principle of relativity. All religious truth must be relative. They must have shifting expressions in different times. The Bible contains witness to the piety and faith of that age. It is completely obvious that we today must look at that matter in a different way.

This way of looking at things also makes the Gospel into just what the Bible calls a heresy: a meaning, a current, a time-bound way of looking at things. Then, the Gospel is in no way what the Early Church meant, when it called it "the Way." It becomes the opposite. One rejects the expression, the thoughts, and the conviction that lie behind the Early Church's self-designation. The Church that knows itself to be "the Way" lives in just this conviction, that it owns the truth, that it owns it so clearly and definitively that it can show the way, not only for its age, but for all people in every age, not only a thoughtful way that fits for some, but the only way, that which all must take.

Against this New Testament faith, modern religiosity places its dogma that everything shifts and changes and that even Christendom must develop. Therefore, it isn't any wonder that this present debate in the Church is so confused. Men can, of course, draw completely contrary conclusions from the same facts. When it can be established that Paul believed and meant one thing and adduced his Lord's command, then the matter is decided about what he believed according to the revelation given at that time. But the relativist answers, yes Paul, yes, at that time. But now?! For him it is not an argument that all past generations read the Bible in a certain manner and that there was only one answer found to this question, because this answer is no longer accepted by a broad secularized opinion. To the contrary, he finds it very natural that a thought or a regulation that is two thousand years old must now be ripe for revision and change. While the way for the one is staked out and given in and with the revelation in Christ, so it is for the other a developing and changing way, where we must grope and seek out new forms of life, also in the world of faith.

In actual fact, this arrangement and this opposition have always been found in the Church's history. They who oppose that once given have certainly come forward in many different forms: as Gnostics, as Platonists, as mystics, as schwarmerei, as Unitarians, as liberal theologians, as champions for the Gospel's "demystification." This is completely natural. Every age has its heresy—or heresies. For a heresy is, of course, a human opinion, the expression of that age's human thoughts. What they all have in common is that they all start from the general revelation of the divine. This means tying together the fashionable thoughts of the age with certain fragments of the Gospel that are found to be compatible with the enlightened ideas of the age.

Against all this has stood throughout time "the faith which was once delivered to the saints," that which the apostle found the urgency to admonish his fellow Christians to fight for. And it isn't any different today. Christendom is "the Way." The Church's way is also staked out. And the Church shall faithfully follow this way where the Lord has gone before.

What does that mean concretely?

Because "the Way" is staked out in the Word, it means to be faithful to the Word, both the broad and the deep.

Broadly: The Word must be able to cover all that touches it in our own day. Biblical faithfulness does not mean repristination of yesterday's theology. There is something that changes and grows. It is not the Word, not the revelation. But it is the situation in which we men live. We cannot just refer to the answers that past generations found in the Bible to their questions. We must seek to find if the answer really is the answer for the question that burns in us. Among these, the questions concerning sin and forgiveness, the certainty of salvation, and the hope for eternal life remain the same. But the questions become in part new. Where Luther met his day's questions—the relationship between the husband and his household, the servants and farmhands, the prince and his subjects, questions for serfs, apprentices, and journeymen—we meet questions of trade unions and employers, individually and collectively, statesmen and the state, the voter and his government. Where Luther wrestles with the question of the Turk and the threat against Christendom, there we have the atom bomb and the threat of total annihilation. All this must be seen in light of the Word. The Bible is God's Word to all ages, also to ours. If anyone has the right to say, "*Nil humani a me alienum puto*" ("I am not a stranger to humanity"), it is Christ, who became true man, who bore all humanity's sin as His own and who won a redemption that applies to every age. All is under Him. This means in every generation that all shall be drawn before Him, illuminated by His Gospel, and subsumed under His authority. It is this that has been forgotten so often. It is noteworthy how little theology, Christian thinking, and Christian proclamation has been occupied with the world's situation today. Certainly it is discussed even within the Church if we should have nuclear weapons or not, if we shall be neutral or not. But for a Christian it also ought to be obvious that the problems have other aspects and that the New Testament has something to say that the world has no idea about. We have no promise of a millennium. God has set an end to history. The course of the world goes to its dramatic end. The evil one mobilizes his last resources, but Christ is victorious in the midst of catastrophe, and the time is short.

This is the Word's broad sphere of influence; it spans over all of life, and it is not only the task of the theologian. It is a highly personal thing for every Christian. It applies to my own private life, my employment, my familial relationships, my hobbies. When a Christian takes all this to his Bible, when he allows the Word to speak about it and constantly anew expects God's answers to his everyday questions so that all this is tied inseparably together with his relationship to Christ, with the forgiveness that he has received for nothing, with the mercy that for Jesus' sake is new every morning, with the justification that makes it possible for such a sinner to be a child of God, yes he is "the Way." He is a living member in the Church that is "the Way."

But there is not only needed a broadening out over every day and all its reality. There is also needed a faith in the deep.

The Scripture's answers do not always lie on the surface. The Scriptures are an organic unity. The ability to read them rightly and understand what one reads hangs together therefore with the insight one has in the Scripture's great connection. This connection has its center, its heart, its inner meaning in Christ. Luther did not understand Scripture until he understood Christ. And he understood Christ when he understood justification by faith was for everyone. So long as he attempted to understand and apply everything from moralism's obvious foundational dogma—namely that we through our obedience and fear of God must be completely changed, must in some manner show our goodwill and make ourselves worthy of God's benevolence—then he misunderstood all: conversion, forgiveness, and sanctification. But when he realized that justification from God was Christ's justification and not ours, and all this was a gift, not a reward, undeserved but real, the only basis for the sinner's forgiveness, then everything was clear. First the truth of salvation and then gradually the Christian view concerning the Church, work, and the family.

This is repeated in every age. Men come to the Divine Service and engage themselves in the Church's work. They have with themselves all our time's obvious dogmas. Most interpret everything in the categories of moralism. But if they are willing to listen, if the preaching and instruction are right and they receive the Word as God's Word, then the connection becomes clear. The essentials about sin and grace have been said with such classic clarity of the Reformers that every man must come to understand it.

But even here it is true that every time has its new situations. To be a sinner who lives by grace is essentially the same now as then, but the world in which the sinners live is different. To be able to properly navigate all these new situations, one needs this deep anchorage in the Bible's whole message. There is a Christian experience, entrusted by the Word, that he reads and grounds himself to, he tests himself by the Word and takes it to heart as it is heard and spoken in continually new connections, and finally he knows it so well that one instinctively conceives what must be right or wrong in very new situations.

This deepening is both an individual and a theological matter. It is, of course, the theologian's task on the one hand to penetrate the Word and understand it in its historical connection and in its factual, original meaning and on the other hand to be able to say what its actual meaning is today.

It is through such faithfulness to the Word, both in the broad and in the deep, that the Church can be "the Way." "The Way" is not comfortable. It is narrow. It may never be the majority's way. Few are they who find it. It is not popular. It is enough for the disciple, if it goes for him as for his Master. But, and here I finish with the word of the prophet:

> And a highway shall be there,
> and it shall be called the Way of Holiness;
> the unclean shall not pass over it.
> It shall belong to those who walk on the *way*;
> even if they are fools, they shall not go astray. (Isa. 35:8 ESV, emphasis added)

WITH ALL BOLDNESS

Pastoral Conference, 1963

"With all boldness..."
There rings an appeal in these words that we know that we need, or perhaps a hint about a help and a concealed asset that we need more than all appeals. We are reminded that they are gathered out of Scripture. But where is it really?

We take a concordance. It belongs to the pastor's most useful books. Sometimes it is quite exciting to read it. It enlightens us that there are three places where the words "all boldness" appear, one in the beginning of Acts, a second in the conclusion of the same book, and a third in the first chapter of Philippians.

Acts 4:29

We begin with Acts 4:29. The context is dramatic. We find ourselves in the weeks after the first Pentecost. There is already a Christian Church in Jerusalem. The first crisis in the relationship to society is brewing. From society's viewpoint the matter ought to be decided. Jesus of Nazareth has been executed, unanimously condemned to death by the land's highest court and the occupation power's representative. His preposterous claim to be the Messiah, God's Son, is refuted. Everything should have returned to the old calm. But the calm is disturbed. It is preached in the temple itself that the one who was lawfully executed lives. People believe it. Inconceivable and highly vexing things are happening. One man who was lame his whole life and whom all saw sit and beg by the Pyle Horaia (the Beautiful Gate), the most used of all the temple's gates, has begun in everyone's sight to walk and allows these Galileans to stand as miracle workers. The police came immediately; they arrested the leaders of the new party and examined them. They had the audacity to stand before the Sanhedrin and say that all this had happened through faith in Jesus—"whom you crucified, whom God raised from the dead" (Acts 4:12a ESV). During the examination, they had summarized the new and preposterous teaching in a pregnant formula: "there is salvation in no one else, for there is no other name under heaven given among men by which we must be saved" (v. 12b ESV). They attempted to handle them with gentle means and only forbade them to speak or teach in Jesus' name. They answered that they could not be silent concerning what they themselves had seen and heard. For this reason they were forbidden even more strictly to speak of this Jesus and then let go.

And now Peter and John too, after their first night in jail, have come back to their own and told what the people's highest court, judging and exercising power with all authority, has made clear for them: that they will not be slapped on the wrist if they attempt to defy this council and their orders any further.

And then? When they heard this, Luke relates, they all cried together to God. It is in this prayer we for the first time encounter the three words "with all boldness." "And now, Lord, look upon their threats and grant to your servants to continue to speak your word with all boldness" (Acts 4:29 ESV).

"With all boldness . . ." There, out before them, lies Jerusalem in the flaming heat of summer days, the city that murders the prophets and stones those who are sent to it. Here one really feels the need to pray for boldness. The Word that one is supposed preach is a challenge to both Jews and Greeks. It is not related to all the other religions that they were otherwise crowded by in the Hellenistic world and that all enjoyed an obvious tolerance. It is not a matter of a religion of the type that constantly grows out of men's longing for the divine and takes form in symbolic myths or philosophical systems. It is a question of fact, about something that has happened here in Jerusalem, which one himself has been a witness to and that has meaning for all men, final meaning, meaning for life and salvation. For the Jews it is an offense, a blasphemy that He who was crucified should be able to be God's Messiah. For the Greeks it is a folly that God would be able to die on the cross. For the Romans it is not worth more than a scornful shoulder shrug already because it comes from these fanatical and unreasonable Jews.

And then, there is the fact. One knows it, and one knows that one may see it and experience it because from the very beginning one has been pointed out to be a witness for God before the world. One knows what is expected. One has heard it many times from the Master's lips: "See, I send you as sheep among wolves." "They will deliver you up to tribulation and put you to death, and you will be hated by all nations for My name's sake." "It is enough for the disciple to be like his teacher." "Do not fear those who can kill the body, and after that there is no more they can do."

And now the hour has also come. One knew it before. Yet does it feel harder than one thought it would? Acts wastes no words on such feelings. But it says that they prayed, and they prayed for boldness.

The word boldness is *parresia* in Greek. This Greek word means more than its Swedish counterpart. The basic meaning is "to be able to say anything," to be able to speak freely, to venture to step forward with that which one has on his heart. In classic Greek it can be used for the democratic right that we call free speech. It can also mean outspokenness, occasionally with a bit of impertinence. Sometimes, even in the New Testament, it simply indicates that something happens openly or publicly.

This, to be able to speak freely, applies both to God and men. There is a *parresia* before God. "If our conscience does not condemn us, we can have boldness to step before God," John says. It means to be able to venture before God to say like a child, "Abba, Father." It is possible only through the security of redemption, through the forgiveness that revokes and crosses out all that we are in ourselves or have earned in our own ways. For this reason it says in Ephesians 3:12 that we in Christ possess "*parresian kai prosagogen*," the ability to speak openly with God and the ability to go straight to Him. The same thought is found carried out in the famous verse in the fourth chapter of Hebrews: "Since then we have a great high priest who has passed through the heavens, Jesus, the Son of God, let us hold fast our confession. . . . Let us then with confidence [*meta parresias*] draw near to the throne of grace" (vv. 14, 16 ESV). The *parresia* before God would be presumption without redemption. This is an impossibility for a wounded conscience. But it is every Christian's privilege through faith in Jesus. It is to venture to "say all" that we are open also in questions of that which one is ashamed of, to be able to go straight away, to draw near to the throne of grace, to receive mercy and find grace to help at the right time. But before everything it is to be a child of God in Christ Jesus, not slaves but children, heirs with Christ, initiated by God.

When it comes to *parresia* before men, the basic meaning of the word is the same: to be able to dare and say everything. Naturally then, it is a matter of what one will say. For one apostle the answer lies in the Great Commission: "teach them to observe all that I have commanded you." One apostolic *parresia* remains in this, that he preaches all that his Lord has taught him. What he heard whispered in his ear in the closet, that he shall preach from the rooftops. He shall do just that which the Great Council forbade: preach in Jesus' name, proclaiming salvation through faith in Jesus. It is to confess Jesus before men. It also does not do to sweep the offensive points under the rug, to attempt to lock up the religiosity as perhaps time bound, make monotheism and morals the chief points, and cautiously paint Jesus as God's revealer and ethical prototype. The religious situation in the Roman Empire seemed ready for one such program. The time was religiously tolerant. Through the motley mishmash of myths and rites, there was an incentive to faith in the one and only God and a longing after a higher and purer ethic. One groped about for an answer to the question of the final meaning of life in eternity. One held to the summary of general revelation that the Enlightenment seventeen hundred years later would put in the three words: God, virtue, and immortality. It is the summary of the knowledge of God that we men can receive through the common revelation in nature and conscience, in the stars of heaven above me and the moral law in my heart, to speak like Kant. The Roman state pictured itself as understanding and tolerant to all this, but with one caveat: that one unquestionably acknowledged the state's sovereignty and its absolute right, embodied in the cult of Caesar.

But Christendom chose not to adapt itself according to the society in which it would now live. It would have meant betrayal to its own innermost being, the proclamation of Christ. For the Gospel is something more than the summary of God's common revelation. It is the joyful message of God's intervention in the world that gives humanity completely new possibilities to know God and come to Him. This news is not only a better message, a clearer insight than what one thought before. It is a deed, a saving intervention. Or to say as the New Testaments says, "God was in Christ reconciling the world to Himself." The summary of this news being this: believe in Jesus, and you are saved.

The Gospel must therefore be an unhelpful offense for the principled religious relativism that stamped Hellenism—just as it so often stamps our time. The message of Christ's Lordship must get caught up in helpless conflict with the society that could tolerate almost everything in the religious sphere, if only one recognized the state's sovereignty. This conflict is prophesied in Jesus' own proclamation: "Beware of men, for they will deliver you over to courts and flog you in their synagogues, and you will be dragged before governors and kings for my sake, to bear witness before them and the Gentiles" (Matt. 10:17–18 ESV).

Before this conflict, the Gospel gives no promise of success according to the meaning that we insert in that word. It just may be that the one who acknowledges Jesus will be hated by all and flee from one city to the next. But he who perseveres to the end shall be saved. That is the promise that is given.

Here a comparison can be made with Churchill at the point in England's history that came to be known afterwards in the world as "their finest hour." He promised his people blood, sweat, and tears—and the final victory. One could use these words for the Early Church. It was the promise one then lived with: blood, sweat, and tears and the final victory. The difference was only this, that the final victory for the lonely fighting Brits in 1941 was still something that they could hope to experience within a few years, see with their eyes, rejoice over like a palpable and undeniable fruit of their sacrifice. For the apostles and the Early Church, it was the final victory, Christ's victory, the new age, something that was so much more than anyone could have ever dreamt of here in time. All hung on this: that He was God's Son, risen from the dead, sitting at the right hand of God the Father Almighty, from thence He will come again to judge the living and the dead.

In this situation, to have *parresia*, boldness, requires that one does not figure that what he now says, does, suffers, and works for will necessarily result in men being convinced and believing the Gospel. But it means to know that this is right, that this is true. So it has and will happen, whatever men might say about it. All hangs on faith in this Jesus. His path went from the cross to the resurrection. He who follows Him may count on taking the same path. He may take his cross.

So the situation must have seemed that summer day, 1,930 years ago, when the apostles in the face of threats from their enemies prayed to their Lord that they would be able to proclaim His Word with all boldness.

Immediately after, Luke continues, "And they continued to speak the word of God with boldness," they followed their program, the program that the Church has since had to follow in every age in the same situations.

How did it go after? The whole program?

Acts 28:31

We turn the pages of history, until we come to the last page of Acts. There in the last verse, we meet the same words again.

Twenty-eight years have passed. Paul, who this time in Jerusalem belonged to the sworn enemies, is now approaching the end of his long trip. He has come to Rome, under guard, in order to receive his sentence. He is met by Christians the moment he steps on land in Puteoli. From Rome, people have gone to meet him at the Three Taverns and Forum Appii, 60 kilometers south on the Via Appia. In Rome he was in custody of the police but still had certain freedom and could rent a home. He lived there for two years. People came and went, he received them, and he wrote letters. "Proclaiming the kingdom of God and teaching about the Lord Jesus Christ with all boldness and without hindrance."

Such is the abrupt end of Acts that has given rise to so many speculations. We leave them there and note only that here again we have the three words: "with all boldness."

In order to understand them, we must attempt to think of what it would be like to be in that stream of people who seek him in the home he rented in one of the numerous Roman apartment buildings, up to six stories high, built of thin Roman brick, not all that safe from collapse (they did that later under Flavious), with endless stairs and no chimneys so that the smoke from the many kitchens had to vent through the windows. In the stairs stood a legionnaire, provided he hadn't gone down to the tavern for a refreshment in the well-founded belief that this prisoner would not make any attempt to escape. Many people have passed through these stairs in the last few days. In the beginning there were great crowds of Jews who wanted to hear what their learned compatriot had to say. They have thinned out now. Some of them belong to his conspiring opponents. There may be complications with him.

In Iconium and Lystra, in Thessalonnia and Corinth, the opposition led to riots and abuse. In Lystra he was stoned and tossed out of the city as dead. It was only one episode in the series. Paul himself had some years earlier made up an apparently quite comprehensive list. It takes up over a half column in a Swedish Bible, a strangely parallel piece to the merit lists that accompany our employment applications. He says that he himself bears the wounds of Christ on his body. Perhaps he means all the honor. He who had not only been stoned but had been publicly flogged eight times, he bore the marks of it throughout his life. Naturally, one can see the marks of a quarter century of toil and drudgery, trips and adventures, vigils, cold, and hunger—not to speak of the stress of being overburdened. This is noticeable even here in Rome, where messengers are coming and going with reports from Ephesus and Colossae, from Antioch and Jerusalem, where as naturally as always, greetings of all kinds are dampened with all types of distress and hardships, persecutions, waste, and division crying out in pain.

Should we ask Paul how in the midst of all this he will continue with all boldness, he might look surprised. He has never thought anything else. It was done so from the beginning. The time when he sat blind in Damascus, the Lord had come to Ananias and commanded him with a greeting: "This man is a chosen instrument for Me. And I shall show him how much he must suffer for My name's sake." Paul is fully prepared to come here to continue, if it doesn't get any worse. The deadly truth has followed him ever since he went up to Jerusalem. He is probably more surprised over how it came to be that there was so much future, that from his point of view he has been allowed to experience it as a final victory day. But this is also natural for him. He had said it some years earlier in a letter to Rome. To be Christian is on the one hand to be treated like sheep to slaughter: "for your sake we are being killed all the day long." And yet: "in all this we win a glorious victory through Him who has loved us."

Philippians 1:20

Perhaps Paul sits down just now and writes about this thing. In all likelihood, Philippians was written during this year in Rome. Here, for the third time, we encounter the words "with all boldness."

It is in the beginning of the letter where he describes his situation, prepared to depart and prepared to stay. "It is my eager expectation and hope that I will not be at all ashamed, but that with full courage [all boldness] now as always Christ will be honored in my body, whether by life or by death" (Phil. 1:20 ESV).

It is instructive here to see what Paul puts in opposition to proclaiming Christ with all boldness. It is to be ashamed. By shame, the apostle does not mean how he was beaten or laughed at, scourged or executed. By shame he means being silent. If he compromises and cuts out some of the offensive aspects in the message about Christ, then Christ is no longer glorified. It is the same thought that he developed in another place, in 2 Corinthians. There he speaks about how God carried him forward in triumph and through him spread His knowledge as a pleasing aroma everywhere, just as the aroma of the censer envelops a procession that proceeds along the Via Sacra. Is that too much to say, is that not presumption? Paul hesitates like others and asks, "Who is sufficient for these things?" (2 Cor. 2:16 ESV). And the answer is this: "For we are not, like so many, peddlers of God's Word, but as men of sincerity, as commissioned by God, in the sight of God we speak in Christ" (v. 17 ESV).

Here again we encounter the apostolic certainty of having been entrusted with a message that cannot be changed. Just as Paul himself has received it as something that went contrary to what he had thought and wished before, so he is guilty of being an ambassador, who does not change or keep secret one word of that which he has been tasked to speak. He speaks before God. He knows who must take responsibility for that which will now happen. Therefore he speaks with parresia all that he has been commanded to say.

And that he does so also means, according to the verse just mentioned in Philippians, that Christ be glorified, now as always. Perhaps it can be a bit presumptuous again, but not from Paul's mouth. He knows what it costs to be Christ's herald. He bears the marks of it all over his body. But this is that manner in which Christ shall be brought out into the world and be glorified, praised, made great before men as the word means. "For we who live are always being given over to death for Jesus' sake, so that the life of Jesus also may be manifested in our mortal flesh" (2 Cor. 4:11 ESV).

So we wonder here why Paul, as so often, changes the wonderful expression, that Christ with all boldness shall be glorified in his body. When this tired and worn, scarred and crippled body that is now, to crown everything, bound in chains, when it can still be used in the Lord's service, when he sits here and dictates, when he receives people, comforts and warns and gives advice, when he instructs and preaches, when the work drags out long into the night's late hours and begins again before the first street vendors have woken or some of the small stalls down on the street have rolled up their windows of wood slats, it is then that Christ is glorified.

And here the great apostle, human, and Christian comes close to his little brothers in the Swedish priesthood, for whom it also means to persevere with all boldness. The basis for boldness is, of course, the same: not some guarantee that it pays off if you figure statistics or weigh on the scale of church politics, but simply this, that He is with us every day until the end of time, He to whom all power in heaven and on earth has been given.

The prisoners are also the same, these whom Paul calls "to forsake their righteousness and purity before Christ." They are imprisoned when Christ is made into something other than He is to fit into a religiosity that is monotheistic, believes in salvation through moralism, and only knows the truth as relative. Or the prison can be faithfulness. One finally wants to escape, finally get some peace, to finally get away from the tension that it costs to serve Him who has been placed as a sign of opposition. Even Paul has known this prison. One sees it already in the oldest of his preserved letters, 1 Thessalonians, where he writes, "But though we had already suffered and been shamefully treated at Philippi, as you know, we had boldness in our God to declare to you the gospel of God in the midst of much conflict" (1 Thess. 2:2 ESV).

Much conflict and still boldness in God, so it is in the apostle's wake. And Paul says in the same breath who it is that gives him boldness amidst much conflict. It is the word that every pastor in every time ought to be able to write of his heart: "For our appeal does not spring from error or impurity or any attempt to deceive, but just as we have been approved by God to be entrusted with the gospel, so we speak, not to please man, but to please God who tests our hearts" (1 Thess. 2:3–4 ESV).

TO PREACH JUSTIFICATION BY FAITH

Tota haec doctrina ad illud certamen perterrefactae conscientiae referenda est, nec sine illo certamine intelligi postest (For the whole of this teaching hangs together with the fight, which a tortured conscience has to endure, and without such a fight cannot understand).

So it is written in the Confessio Augustana (XX). It is concerned with the teaching of justification by faith: the whole of this doctrine belongs together with the fight that a tortured conscience has to endure, and which it cannot understand without such a fight.

This wise word speaks from the Reformers' deepest experience. We ought to always remember it if we are to be able to make the doctrine of justification by faith living for our time and preach it so that men of our age can understand it.

As is known, this question was the topic of discussion at the Lutheran World Federation's conference in Helsinki in the fall [of 1963]. The attempt to interpret it in new terms and metaphors failed. One could not find any formula that satisfied everyone. And I believe that the failure was in large part because for too many it was not clear that this article cannot be understood if one has not felt what the Augustana calls a tortured conscience's fight, also man's agony under God's judgment, that judgment that he feels as just and right. On the contrary, it appeared often enough as if one believed that the doctrine of justification must obviously be able to make itself real and living for a "modern man." And a modern man is conceived of as a man who no longer looks for a gracious God but at most for the meaning of life. Now if one wants to meet this person on his own terms, then it is not incredible that the teaching of justification must find a new presentation that makes it unrecognizable to the rest of us.

It is therefore important that we begin by noting what the Augustana says: this teaching cannot be understood by those who have no idea of the tortured conscience's fight and unrest. There are then many men who have no chance of understanding it. If there are particularly many such men today, then it should be investigated as to why this is.

Here, it is not hard to find the answer. Some don't believe in any god above their head. Others have a dim concept of Him, in which it goes without saying that He is good and loves to forgive us if we might find ourselves in some need of forgiveness.

Such men do not encounter any qualms of conscience, and they have therefore—according to the Augustana—no chance of understanding what the righteousness of faith is. There is no reason to try explain it to them. One has to take a different starting point. One must try get them to see what they have as of yet failed to understand: God's holiness, His sovereign right to us, our responsibility before Him, His fatherly care and longing after us, and our duty to thank and love, obey and serve Him.

With that I will go to the first point of what I have to say.

1. To Preach the Righteousness of Faith, We Must Preach God's Righteousness and Holiness.

If men have not received a correct picture of God's holiness, they cannot understand the righteousness of faith. The false picture of an all-seeing, generous, and tolerant God, who has the profession of forgiving, as Voltaire says, makes it hard or impossible for a man to understand the real Gospel. This false picture of God is common today. It belongs to the common folk religion of our day's zeitgeist [Utgestaltning]. Natural religion in times past and among other people has often been associated with the fear of God and His wrath. This is understandable because one of its most important sources of the natural revelation is the conscience. Among heathens one often finds a dull, imprecise fear of the god whose judgment we men have the capacity to experience precisely because we are men. But among evangelical people, there seems to be a misunderstanding and possibly an incorrect proclamation that the Gospel has taken away even this natural knowledge of God. God's love has been preached so much and in such a way that for many people it has become a banal and uninteresting self-evident fact that God is good, that He forgives, that we have nothing to fear from that area, if there even is a God.

In this situation one must seriously and thoroughly proclaim the whole truth about God: that His being is love and holiness, that it is this that is an explanation of His actions. His holiness is incompatible with sin (or perhaps it is better to say it concretely: incompatible with all that is petty and self-serving, impure and untrue, self-serving and heartless). To try and come to God with un-atoned for sin is like putting a piece of paper in an open fire. And it is all of God's being, also His love, which is a burning fire for all that is impure. But at the same time, God longs in His love after His children. He seeks us and draws near to us, but we reel back when we understand who He is and what He wants. Men can say that they do not understand talk of sin all they want, but still they reel back before the Lord's Supper. There, they can choose not to come. But he who cannot yet come before God here on earth, how can he do it in eternity?

So in all appropriate contexts, and this needs to be done in almost every sermon, we have to attempt to bring out some of the features of God's true being: endless love and incorruptible holiness. It means for example that we must preach God's Law not only in connection with different spheres of life but constantly anew in all His demands on all of men. I don't believe there is anything that can make it clear for a common religious person that she is a sinner better than the constant reminder of the first and foremost commandment: to love God above all things. If we can constantly make that commandment live anew over the second greatest—to love your neighbor as yourself—and concretely show how we also ought to be, then men will begin to say to themselves, "But I am not that way." We ought be overflowing with a joyful willingness to always serve God. We ought to have Him before our eyes in everything. We ought to overflow with a generous love, that applies to all men, that never tires of them, that never takes offense at them. But we are not that way.

To a certain extent here, one can count on the anonymous Law that men do not always know as God's Law but still holds them under pressure that they sometimes experience as a bondage and partly as guilt. God is also found in creation, also in society and this demand for holy living and a particular way of acting. Many men sigh under this demand that they don't feel they live up to. They are not so effective in their work, not so good and friendly at home, not so glad and helpful in company as they know they ought to be. They thereby end up in something that can be a form of bondage under the Law. We shall not exaggerate this, and we shall be wary of saying in an oversimplified way that God meets us also in the ordinary things of human life. It can be the devil we encounter there. But we are right to say this when men put this demand on each other and on themselves and want to be helpful and noble. So it happens therefore that God's Law is written in all men's hearts. It is completely correct that we ought to be this way. It is correct that we know that something is wrong when we are not that way. God has every right to demand all of this from us. There is no escape from this situation if one does not receive another factor, the Gospel of Jesus Christ.

2. In Order to Preach about Justification by Faith Properly, We Must Instruct Properly about the Righteousness of Works.

We must make it clear that there is a righteousness that God demands of us. This we have already said. We may not speak in such a way about sin that it becomes an abstraction. God's will always touches our daily reality, and this is what we have to help men see. Therefore, the Bible contains so much about parenting, and this element cannot be removed from our preaching. It shall not just be said that our faith should show itself in everyday life. Something must be said about how it shows itself. But then it is so important that the background is clear. Men must learn to understand that there is an outward righteousness that we can and ought to perform.

We might at some point make it clear that this outer righteousness, for the most part, is something that can be performed even by those who do not believe, but still do the Law's work as it is written in his heart. He might certainly have pulled it off better if he had believed, but what he accomplishes might also outshine what a believer with the same natural equipment, with fewer pounds, is lucky to accomplish.

This outward obedience and righteousness has its place here in time, just as it is praised in the Fourth Commandment and as experience confirms: honesty is the best. When everyone attends his occupation, then whatever we encounter goes well.

But this righteousness is not the same as righteousness before God. Righteousness before God means to be able to stand for questioning before all God's Law and say, "Lord, all this I have kept." If one wants to express it in a simple manner for people, he can say that to be righteous is to be finished with the court, so finished that nothing is taken, not the least before God. And now, a simple and concrete instruction on the two commandments of love continually anew must be made clear for our consciences here, that we are not finished, neither do we meet the mark. But neither should we preach against the middle-class righteousness, as if it were not worth anything. It doesn't do to put it forward as ideal self-righteousness or attempt to show that it is only inward selfishness, and call it hypocrisy. It should be given the honor it should have, and one can also calmly continue to keep speaking at congregation members' birthdays and thank them for their deeds, even if this only applies to the communal and middle-class areas, but one shall simultaneously preach the Law so that it does what Scripture says: every mouth is stopped and the whole world stands guilty before God. An accuser is not needed for this. Warmhearted talk about what it means to love, how we ought to be, about the relationship with those who ask for a loan, and about never using an angry word of abuse or a vain word work well.

This proclamation of the higher righteousness must then be united with a realistic description of how we all fall short. This description should be merciful but not smoothed over. It may not be so light as if it were self-evident that we cannot accomplish this and just as self-evident that God still loves us. But it must describe how we with every reason experience this failure as a humiliation, a beat down, a shame. Here, it can be gladly spoken of how the conscience accuses us and how we question ourselves about whether we can even be Christian, if God could really have anything to do with us, if there is something unhelpfully wrong with us, because of which we are never able to receive a right hearing no matter how much we pray about it. And it shall be declared that what is most wrong with us is the hereditary corruption of our nature, original sin, that which Scripture calls the flesh, and that which notes soberly that it neither can nor wants to be submissive to God's Law.

It is important that this is said with pastoral care, with the background of a concrete description of our need. These truths will scarcely hit home if they come as an accusation against civic righteousness and condemn what men might have experienced as the most important and best they have done. It must be built up in living proclamation of the love that God expects of us, a graphic and realistic description of our failure when we attempt to accomplish it. Here, the pastor can speak in the first person to make it known that it applies to all, even us pastors.

If we have gotten this far, the doors are open for the Gospel and we now say furthermore:

3. In Order to Preach Justification by Faith, We Must Preach Correctly Concerning Christ.

This preaching must continuously run parallel with the proclamation of God's holiness, His Law, our guilt, and our sinful depravity. When men need Christ, His picture ought to be there already. It is probable that they will give little attention to what we said about the Savior and his work so long as they do not really need him. But it is still important that all that is said about Christ helps to give a living and right picture of Him. This means not only preaching about His work of redemption. It is central and it must be driven with perseverance and care. But it must have its background in all that we say about Christ's person, His proclamation, His manner of dealing with sinners, His resurrection, and His second coming. With every hearing, our proclamation ought to gradually build up a living picture of God's own Son, who was put under the Law that we broke and fulfilled it all, so that He stands there as the only righteous one. It ought to be clear for all how he is God's righteousness and God's love, who comes here to seek and save those who were lost. So it also ought to be made clear to everyone why He had to die, why there is not some other way out than that He take up our guilt and bear our sins in His body up on the tree of the cross. In Him sin was united with God in the only way that it is possible: God's holiness condemned and consumed it, but the judgment affected Him who took it upon Himself. And now we come to the chief point.

4. To Preach Justification Is to Point to This Christ and in God's Name Proclaim That Everyone Who Believes in Him Receives Forgiveness for All Their Sins.

One shall also not preach justification by faith by pointing to God's love and His fatherly goodness to us. There is a clear tendency to this, not the least in German theology, also in a portion of the document from the Lutheran World Federation. One might say "God's Love in Christ" and ask men to believe in it. But it is precisely this that doesn't work, in any case not so that it becomes a true faith, if one does not explain what God's love did when God gave His only Son and let Him die for our sake and in our place.

If one then has rightly preached Christ, then one can point to Him and bid all burdened sinners to believe in Him. According to the old tradition in the West Coast, it shall be done at least once in every sermon, namely in the second part of the application. It is a good custom. It guarantees that the most important is covered every Sunday. But naturally one can and ought, as Schartau and the fathers, also otherwise talk about this. One shall not tire of it should it seem as if men will not hear it. One can easily get this impression from the congregations, which in great extent are composed of men with poor knowledge and irregular church habits. One can there see how they listen when one talks about God and us, of God's power and demand, of our responsibility, of our endeavors and failures. But when one speaks comfort to the awakened, men begin to squirm. This cannot lead us to strike this from our sermons. One may, at least, lay the emphasis more on that which belongs to preparation and if we have spoken on this before. But the most important must always be there. The day will come when men need it. If there was only one in the church today that needed it, that is enough reason to speak of it with warmth and care.

I said that we preach justification by faith by pointing to Christ, the Redeemer, and in God's name offer the forgiveness of sins to all who believe in Him. This is not just a teaching we lay out. Here we stand as God's ambassadors, in the highest degree, and offer the forgiveness of sins in His name. Here God works, awakens faith, forgives sins. Every proclaimer, just as every listener, knows that one can comprehend something of this in the stillness of the Church.

It also belongs to this preaching to be able to say something about the essence of faith—that it is our emptiness, our need, our outstretched hand—and then about Christ who comes to us and fills this emptiness. Faith is a cloud where Christ lives, says Luther. Men probably understand justification best if one uses the picture of the exchange between me and Christ, where Christ takes all my guilt, punishment, shame, and death and in its place gives me His righteousness, His holiness, His glory, and His life. Even the picture of the precious clothes which cover up the lost son's dirty rags makes it possible to explain what it means that Christ's righteousness is an imputed righteousness, another's righteousness, not our own, not that which we attain through our obedience and repentance.

Finally,

5. To Preach Justification by Faith Is to Make It Clear That He Who Believes That He Possesses Some of His Own Righteousness Has No Standing before God.

Justification by faith is Christ's righteousness. Just as I have no eternal life that does not come from Christ, so have I no righteousness. A believing man remains an old Adam and a new man. The old Adam remains. He can be crucified, but he cannot be changed. He comes to plague us with thoughts of repudiation and shameful proposals. He can do it in the most sacred moment, even at the Lord's Supper. But at the same time, Christ is there, in whom I believe. There is a new man who believes in Him and has the will to serve Him. Therefore, a Christian must experience his existence as a fight, as a conflict. Therefore, we are always sinners, for even the old Adam is a part of ourselves, of our own ego. He is involved in everything, and we need forgiveness in every moment and for all we do and are.

I pass over here, for the sake of time, the question of how justification by faith should be preached to saints. The matter will be covered if only to say that if we preach Law and Gospel right, then men are not drawn by grace to dissolution. The real guarantee is not some teaching but this fact that Christ Himself is in those who believe. And where Christ is and the disciples live before His face, there the whole of the disciples' lives will be different. These are interconnected.

A Few More Short Remarks.

Justification is not a matter that one hits upon one or two Sundays a year. It is a theme that must permeate all our sermons. It must be built, be explained, be made clear, deepened, repeated, and drummed in Sunday after Sunday.

Finally, it is not a doctrine. Here God works through His Word. That God really works is in the assumption that men shall be able to take this message and understand the teaching. It serves nothing to attempt to explain it for men, who know nothing of the conscience's distress and his own guilt. If it is true, as it says in the document from Helsinki, that modern man really doesn't ask for a God of grace, the Church has no reason to try think of how one should form a message of justification so that it can also be accepted by he who does not need God's grace. Rather, we have reason to seek what it is that takes hold of this so-called modern man and makes it so that he does not understand his situation.

"For the whole of this teaching hangs together with the fight, which a tortured conscience has to endure, and without such a fight cannot understand."

But where God comes near us in judgment and grace, there He can be understood. And that God shall come near us, it is the meaning of all our work in the Church. It is not our task to try find new formulas that can let us and our hearers pass by the judgment of our sins. But may we pray for grace to be able to rightly extend that which is our real task: to so preach God's Word with such spirit that it leads to confession of sin and to a firm and sanctifying faith in Christ.

THE MESSAGE FROM THE UNKNOWN

Pastoral Conference, 1965

> "What you therefore worship as unknown, I now proclaim to you . . ."
> —Acts 17:23

We remember the word. Paul had come to Athens for the first time in his life. He had gone around and looked at the celebrated city, which from its early greatness had now sunk to being something like Jena or Heidelberg, a university city for the sons of rich people, aesthetes, and philosophers. Paul considered how the whole city was filled with idols, and he, not without reason, was upset to find the whole divine court of Olympus with all these adventurous characters, mixed with the Orient's strange animal gods, put forward in this city famed for its fine cultural tradition.

There are certainly substantial similarities between that era of Athens and our day in the West. Luke says with a glint of humor: "Now all the Athenians and the foreigners who lived there would spend their time in nothing except telling or hearing something new" (Acts 17:21 ESV). They did not have our evening papers or the hot headlines on the front page, but even there one was aware of the worth of news and knew that the sensational was always viable. Even there they needed to be constantly fed with new sensations combined with a conviction that one needed to follow the times, and the trade in them was the focal point.

In this interest for news, there was also a place for religion. It was open for debate, just like all news. New cults were imported from the East. New ways of thinking were launched from within philosophy. Among all this the Athenians made themselves judges and sat in authority by their ability to rate philosophers, mystagogues, and theologians.

Behind this interest there was also another longing, the human heart's desire for his Creator. It could be so strong that the roles were cast, and men humbly stepped forward as supplicants before the altar and the idols where they found rest. The religiosity that springs from this natural revelation is itself fairly the same in every age. It oscillates between human arrogance that sets itself as judge over the divine and a restless worship that seeks after means to humor the divine and win its favor. Sometimes it sinks down to magic that consists of a false sense between reaching for the unknown powers and the feeling of being their lord. The ancient world was full of such magicians with their differing forms of witchcraft, books of the black arts, and amulets. There was a more cautious religion among the sacrificing and worshiping people. Among the intellectuals there was a more noble and spiritualized religiosity like the one pictured. A man like Cicero is not very far away from the eighteenth century's religious enlightenment. Even he could have gathered the essential contents of religion in these three words: God, virtue, and immortality.

Paul now encounters all this in Athens. We know how it went. Paul was led before the Areopagus. Thousands of tourists have stood there in our day and let their eyes sweep up to the Parthenon or down to the Agora. Now, one wants to know what this new teaching that he proclaimed was about. It was new; it was also very interesting. One wants to know, and one was also very convinced of his ability to judge between different religions. At the same time, there was something unsettling and challenging in Paul's word, "for you bring some strange things to our ears."

Paul begins by reporting all that he had seen in Athens. He has determined that the Athenians are a religious people. It has disturbed him to see all their idols, but that is not all he says. He sees through the distortion in this perversion of common religiosity. All these idols embody the god that one made himself, and therefore in the end he lords over the god. It is a god that one approaches with demands and achievements: do ut des. (Quid quo pro. You scratch my back, I'll scratch yours.) If the gods did not fulfill what one expected of them, one could throw them to the ground and smash them to pieces, just like folk religion does even today when one approaches God with his particular demand and throws Him away when He doesn't fulfill them.

What does Paul do?

His manner of speaking is an important lesson for us pastors, who all encounter a similar folk religion. To summarize Paul's speech in the Areopagus, one could use the words "what you worship as unknown, this I proclaim to you."

These words put everything in the right place. Here is what the religiosity is in the city. This religiosity consists not only of mistakes. This is there because there is a God. God has made Himself known in His creation and through the conscience of man. But through this natural revelation, He allows only the thought. He is the completely unknown God.

But from this unknown God comes a new message. He reveals Himself. He has stepped into the world and operated. And now He speaks through His envoys, the servants of the Word.

This is the pastor's situation, his joyful situation. There is always some thought about the God that has been revealed in His work ever since creation. For this reason there is also an interest in religion. Those who have it really hard are not the proclaimers of the Gospel, but atheists. Men are by nature religious. The question of God constantly pops up.

And here the pastor may now speak to this situation, where God already is. And the pastor knows that he has a message that hits home, that answers something in man's nature. There is a sense, a longing, a need, and a questioning. That which works to all this is the same God who now speaks. The unknown God from whom the pastor comes with a message, He is simultaneously the one who brought about this notion. The Unknown now becomes the Revealed, the dumb becomes the One who speaks.

How does Paul carry this out?

He begins by describing something that we know both through the natural revelation and the particular. He proceeds also from that which is true in the natural religiosity, that which one can get to by taking hold of the light she already has received. "The God who made the world and everything in it, being Lord of heaven and earth, does not live in temples made by man" (Acts 17:24 ESV). A stoic philosopher could also say all this. And he could have agreed also when Paul continues, "Nor is he served by human hands, as though he needed anything, since he himself gives to all mankind life and breath and everything" (v. 25 ESV).

So much can be drawn out of the revelation that one now encounters all over the world. It belongs to what mankind knows from the beginning and that up to our day lingered as a natural knowledge of God that is often highly intelligent and pure even among the most primitive people in the Kalahari or the Tierra Del Fuego.

But when Paul so invokes the natural revelation, he simultaneously cites the Old Testament without his audience knowing it. Paul is not without reason for doing so. He supports himself not from folk religion—not everything there is right—but from the Word. He has tested all this pious talk and these notions before the Word. Therefore, he knows what is right and what he has the right to say.

And he now uses what is right to critique the false folk religion. He has not thought softly about these temples and idols and about these men who sacrifice there. He knows that they come with their gifts to he who has the power to get him over to his side. Now he places his critique here: "God does not live in temples that are made with hands, neither does He need to be served by us men as if He were in need of anything."

So Paul takes his starting point in the folk religion, but from the very beginning draws a clear line between that which is true and false, between that which is divine revelation and that which is simply human additions and speculations. He draws the line without attacking his audience. He puts them to the test without saying, "Such are you, and so it applies to you." He says instead, "Such is God, so great, so powerful." He knows that he notes something that they themselves have been able to think. From there he draws the conclusion: neither does He need any of our gifts.

In all this lies a deep wisdom. Not the least in the starting point: to not attack wrongs without first noting what is right. This is not just the captatio benevolentiae that the antique rhetoricians recommended as introduction to every speech. But it is to know God's work and hold fast to it. God has already been here among these people. Therefore, there is something that precedes him.

So Paul continues with a contemplation concerning this natural revelation. But we can pass over that here. From there he goes over to the great message, that which has been revealed through God's intervention in the world. What Paul had said before, he has said to help the audience understand their situation with their own religion, both that which is right in it and that which is complete human speculation. Now, the crucial word comes, that God-given answer to the question of human longing. The living God intervenes, acts here on earth, and sends His redemptive Word to His children. To this situation, he expresses the matter in this way: "The times of ignorance God overlooked, but now he commands all people everywhere to repent, because he has fixed a day on which he will judge the world in righteousness by a man whom he has appointed; and of this he has given assurance to all by raising him from the dead" (Acts 17:30–31 ESV).

Luke's narration naturally gives us a suggestive summary, but he gives the essentials. Now, God has intervened—He has said and done the crucial. Now He bids all these, His created children, in all lands and people that turn to Him. He has ordained a Savior, before whom every human destiny is now determined for life or death. All this He has demonstrated by raising Him from the dead.

Now notice that Paul in no way derives this message out of the premises of folk religion. He does not appeal to his audience to give him some correct starting point that they already thought and are ready to keep. The essential and crucial is something new, something that happened in conflict with all that one could expect and something that can now be proclaimed and shall be received in faith.

Paul only starts from the natural revelation to show man's situation and to get the audience to recognize it again. He deepens natural revelation and purifies it. God is already here, we live in Him, and it is from this we get our thought and longing. But Paul does not build on all this when he gets to the essentials. He only makes sure that they do not draw some other conclusions than what can be drawn, namely that coarse idolatry must not be right. There are other such conclusions. They can be drawn from the conscience and our sense of unfulfilled obligations, our ambitions, and our feeling of falling short.

Such can help us to understand that we always stand guilty before God and cannot answer Him for one in a thousand. But when it comes to the answer, the Gospel message, then Paul draws no conclusions from what the audience already knew. Instead, he started from a completely new message. And he did it with boldness and joy. He knew that he had a redemptive word to say.

This can be an important lesson for us pastors. It is a common mistake, often committed during this century, to seek a bond with the religiosity before the Gospel's untilled land and attempt to make it understood by leveraging folk religion without seriously taking it any further. This manner of preaching has grown out of a feeling that is right in and of itself. Such preaching never grabs hold of a congregation where the majority don't question folk religion. It may now be at a Christmas service, a confirmation, a devotional hour in a company, in rotary, or some other situation. The preacher has during preparation asked himself: what can people understand from this text? What is it that is in line with their daily lives and experience? The answer is regularly something that falls within the realm of folk religion. It can be such as has to do with God's existence, His providence, care, and fatherly love. It can be moral questions and such as regulate our day. For this reason these proclamations too often smack of deism and moralism. It can begin already in Sunday School, and it can continue in the same manner for the whole life, right up to burial.

If we ask how it comes that men so often believe that folk religion is the same as Christendom, so have we here one of the reasons. The proclamation attempts to make an affiliation but makes it in a false manner. "To speak in a manner as men understand" can be really dangerous. Sometimes it gets a bit slippery when it comes to the line that lies within their horizon, when it in fact lies outside. Sometimes one crosses the line but speaks so cautiously that the message doesn't reach home. Perhaps afterwards they say what Paul spoke about: "God has determined a day when He will come to judge the world with righteousness through one man He has appointed." But one has done it with so many strange words about the eschatological final perspective or the double output, or with so many vague hints about love having the last word and that God will be all in all, that no one would understand that there really was any question that he himself might be reprobate.

It is strange how much one can speak about Jesus without breaking the folk religion's frame of understanding: Jesus reflects God's love. He preaches love (also morals and law). He will gather us all after death in His kingdom and even more. Within this frame of understanding, one can fit in a good deal about forgiveness (though not redemption and the forgiveness of sins for Jesus' sake), and a good deal about the Spirit (though not the Spirit who through the Word creates faith in Christ's reconciliation). So one can fool himself and the congregation that it is Christendom one preaches, but in reality it is a folk religion equipped with Christian ethics.

What God here has the right to expect of His messengers is that they shall dare to come with the message from the unknown, that they shall dare to say that which is not found in the folk religion, the new that was not known before, so that people no longer think it is enough that they are religious, and to say that which to the contrary wakes their indignant protests but which is God's power to salvation.

Paul does not always connect to folk religion. From Athens he goes to Corinth. Here he says himself that he will know nothing but Jesus Christ and Him crucified, just that which folk religion doesn't know about. It has been suggested that this was because of the experience in Athens, and that from this one can determine that the chief lesson we should learn from this is not to attempt to find any connection in natural revelation before preaching the Gospel. This lesson will hardly do. Acts does not put forward Paul's preaching at the Aeropagus as an example of what not to do. It is an example of when it is right to make such a connection. But one shall then do as Paul. One goes into the human situation and lets them recognize themselves in his example, in his searching, but at the same time draws up lines between what is right and what is false in the folk religion's conventional and imaginary solutions, to then bring forward the full weight and determination of the message from the Unknown, the Gospel of Jesus Christ.

For the Sundays in Fall, there are many texts that give unsought application to a soul-curing settlement to many of folk religion's fundamental mistakes.

On the Fifteenth Sunday after Trinity, the text encounters Martha and Mary. The answer that this text gives on the important issue goes counter to folk religion's conception. One can let the text speak and avoid any unnecessary polemics. In the introduction one can ask the question, "What is the most important thing in religion?" One can refer to some of the most usual answers: to believe in God, to live right, to follow your conscience and do your best. One can point for point conclude that this is important and that God demands this but that the answer to the question of what is most important, that which can be called the one thing needful, is something completely different. Then let the Lord Christ Himself speak and declare that which is the one thing needful and why this is and must be more important than all else. Thereby the text itself will be a powerful resolution of folk religion's greatest mistake: that the means of grace essentially are not so important and that one can be a Christian without going to church.

On St. Michael's Day, we have the same possibility to let the word correct one of folk religion's most beloved dogmas. The folk religion, certainly unconsciously, usually changes the second text in the children's Gospel so that it means, "for such belong to God's kingdom." Even if the change is unconscious, it is not inconsequential. It gives expression to folk religion's conviction that it must be an obvious right to come into God's kingdom for all kinds of naturally compassionate, benevolent, and guiltless people. The Savior and the conscience can be needed for certain immoral individuals but not for the good and decent people whom He will gladly allow to account for themselves.

Neither here need one begin polemically but can like Paul show the folk religion in their seeking after God. In this case it is our human need of finding a protection and security for our children, these who surely drove some of their mothers to Jesus. Baptism has a strong place in our time with such religious reasons that often feel more at home on the First Article's ground than within the Third and Second. Then the text opens up the gates to truth and shows that essentially it is a question of what Jesus means, what the truth contains, and so on.

Other Sundays one can contemplate if one ought to let folk religion have some connection. When we have to preach about the cripple by Bethesda, one can choose subjects that scarcely touch it. But one could also take up the problem that hangs together with this manner of experiencing sickness. Some treat them without getting out of the frame of folk religion. One can begin by depicting how hard it is to be sick, how completely meaningless it can seem after thirty-eight years, how all the others are self-centered and don't bother to help anyone else, and so on. Then one can say that Christ will always help, and always has time for the forgotten. One can say that He often helps where one least expects it and that one should not forget to thank Him, and so on. The whole time one remains within the frame of folk religion but cautiously passes over the question that is the most burning for folk religion: why is it that so often God doesn't help? Why is there so much trouble and suffering? If one will preach the Gospel from this text, one must dig deeper, God will help, but He will help deeper and longer than men usually think. There is something that is worse than being sick—that which Jesus suggests when He bids the one who has been cured to now repent. For the man at Bethesda, Jesus was still the Unknown. Even among us He often makes men well without them knowing it was Him. But He doesn't always do it. We do not hear that He did it with the others in the five-roofed colonnades. Why not?

Here we must let the Gospel show how God's plan to help all, *even with that which is worse*, demands a completely different course of action. The real evil can only be cured through faith in Jesus. The condition for that to happen is in the text: Jesus met him in the temple. There the Unknown became the Known. That which one thought at one time and was at one time thankful to, He shows Himself now to be the indispensable helper, He who one always has reason to thank.

When Paul had preached in Athens, some people made fun of him, but others said, "We will hear you again about this." So then Paul took leave from the gathering. There were some who kept listening to him and came to faith.

And this is what even we pastors have to count on. No matter how skillfully we connect to that which is right in folk religion, many will scoff at us when we preach the Gospel. The offense and stumbling block that God made when He offered His own Son as an atonement for our sins cannot be spirited away by an older congenial understanding of contemporary life and its people.

There is no surer method of distorting the Gospel than to demand that it shall be preached so "that a modern man can understand it" if one really means by "understanding" the same as "accept." However, it is really that he shall be able to understand it in the meaning that he understands what the issue is, even with the risk that he will be indignant, embittered, and aggressively opposed, even if before he was perhaps indifferent. If some react in this manner, so there is always the other side, just as in Athens, that a few come to faith. And it was for their sake we are sent out with the message from the Unknown.

SHEPHERDS, NOT LORDS

Pastoral Conference, 1967

Those who led medieval parishes used to be called church lords. In many of the parishes, we can still read the names of one or another of them: Lord Johan in Lagaholm, Lord Esbjörn in Skutmansleff, Lord Andreas in Kongahälla, and so on. In Bohuslän they used to be called sire since the Middle Ages, just as they do today in Iceland.

To be called lord was not a usual thing at that time. The title was reserved for noblemen who were simultaneously dubbed knights. On the worldly side, there were also not very many lords in the kingdom. That one such title was born by our parish priests with its own application possibly shows better than anything else the place the Church had in medieval society.

The Reformation opposed this worldly position of power. For Luther it appeared as an unauthorized confusion of spiritual and worldly authority. In the twenty-eighth article of the Augsburg Confession, it says the authority of bishops, which here is similar to the Church's, according to the Gospel consists in the full power to proclaim the Gospel, forgive and retain sins, and administer the Sacraments. This power is carried out only through teaching and proclaiming, baptizing, administering the Lord's Supper, loosing, and binding. They who have been entrusted with the office of Word and Sacrament have no other jurisdiction than to forgive sins, test teachings and reject those teachings that deviate from the Gospel and to exclude manifest sinners from the congregation's Communion. In such things they operate according to God's commission. If they have any other jurisdiction, such as in Luther's time in questions of marriage or tithes, so they have it on grounds of human right and answer to men and have a responsibility to comply with what people determine. When they therefore proclaim God's Word, they answer to

God and may not change a jot or tittle according to their own discretion or because people want it said.

So the Reformers thought. There lies therefore something significant in that the word "church lord" in our land after the Reformation was changed to "church shepherd" (kyrkoherre-kykoherda). One used to suppose it was under the influence of the word *pastor*. In the reformed societies, this has been the usual title and with us it came to be changed in administrative language, legislation, and eventually even in everyday speech. In any case, the development fits well to the Reformation's basis. Priests should be shepherds, not lords.

We all know that the words are taken directly from the New Testament. They occur in their classic place in I Peter that is included in our ordination rite and is the final call that we all receive at the altar on our ordination day: "Shepherd the flock of God that is among you, exercising oversight, not under compulsion, but willingly, as God would have you; not for shameful gain, but eagerly; not domineering over those in your charge, but being examples to the flock. And when the chief Shepherd appears, you will receive the unfading crown of glory" (1 Pet. 5:2–4 ESV).

So we were sent out as shepherds, not as lords. What does this mean?

Here it is already said with great clarity. We have the flock of God in our care. It is then a question of a shepherd's commission, the same as Peter received with the words "be a shepherd for My sheep." That the congregation's shepherds have their commission from God, and that in the authority of that commission they would be the flock's shepherds and caretakers, this was deeply inscribed in the conscience of early Christendom. We meet the same thought, word for word, in Acts 20, in the story about Paul meeting with the pastors in Ephesus. (I say pastors, where the text talks about presbyters, or elders; it is healthy for us to experience the connection in such a place. The distribution of tasks may have taken place over time, but the shepherd's commission remains, and we pastors can apply what the New Testament says to such presbyters word for word to us.) Paul says here as well as elsewhere: "Pay careful attention to yourselves and to all the flock, in which the Holy Spirit has made you overseers, to care for the church of God, which he obtained with his own blood" (Acts 20:28 ESV).

The shepherd really has the flock in their care. He is made an overseer. That is one answer.

But the other is just as important: He is not to lord over the flock. He shall be an example for it. He shall lead and show the way. The shepherd goes ahead, but he is not lord.

Here lies a problem. How can one be a leader and shepherd and have the flock in his care if one is not at the same time lord?

It seems as if it isn't possible. And yet the New Testament says it is so. And for those who are ordained, it is well worth making it clear for them what the Bible has to say about being a shepherd and not a lord.

Not Lords

The New Testament is significantly careful when it comes to using the word *lord*. In bourgeois society it can be used without thinking about the usage of the time. A slave has his lord. The people have their lords, and when one shall be courteous one calls another man "lord." But as soon as he speaks about God's kingdom and God's people, then it is a word reserved exclusively for He who is Lord of lords, even God Himself, and He who from God has received the name that is above all names, namely Lord Christ. "For us there is . . . one Lord, Jesus Christ, through whom are all things and through whom we exist" (1 Cor. 8:6 ESV). He is "our only Master and Lord, Jesus Christ" (Jude 1:4 ESV). This is the only real lordship that a Christian can recognize. Certainly there are earthly lords, and one shall obey and serve them, but one does it—as Colossians's third chapter says—for the Lord's sake, because he wants that: "You are serving the Lord Christ," even when one is serving men.

Also in the parables, where earthly lords occur, looming behind them all is the Lord of lords. As is it with the vineyard's Lord, so it is with the Lord who deposits His capital with His servants and leaves the country. Jesus draws the parallel Himself: "Watch therefore, you know neither the day nor the hour when your Lord comes."

Pastors shall also serve this Lord, just as every other Christian shall serve Him. Just like every other Christian, the pastor also has his particular commission as servant. "Who then is the faithful and wise servant, whom his master has set over his household, to give them their food at the proper time?" (Matt. 24:45 ESV). It is a picture of the pastor's responsibility. He is a servant, but a servant who has been set over his household to give them their food at the proper time, so to fulfill the command "feed My sheep."

A servant who is set over the household, only a servant and then in this connection set over others, in him we meet the problem again: shepherd for God's congregation but not lord over it.

Not lord. What is it he may not be?

Jesus has spoken about it when He shows the great contrast between the foremost in the world and the foremost in God's kingdom. The people's princes step forward as lords over them, and the great men show that it is they who are powerful. They let themselves be called "your grace." They have this power over men, as an officer has over his aide de camp. He says, "Go," so he goes. He says, "Come," so he comes. So it is in the world. You know it is so, Jesus says.

Not So with You

"But not so with you," Jesus says with great emphasis. And He says it to the apostles, to the shepherds of the flock. In His kingdom, the greatest shall be like the youngest and the leader as one who serves.

There is no worse distortion of the shepherd's commission than when one exploits it to play lord. The whole Bible witnesses against this matter. The Old Testament has much to say about the shepherds. Often it then means the people's political leaders, but there was no separation in that case. They too had a commission from God. They would lead the flock, feed them, and seek their best. But it is just that which they did not do. "You eat the fat, you clothe yourselves with the wool, you slaughter the fat ones, but you do not feed the sheep" (Ezek. 34:3 ESV). This is unprecedented: "My shepherds have not searched for my sheep, but the shepherds have fed themselves, and have not fed my sheep" (v. 8 ESV). On the contrary: "with force and harshness you have ruled them" (v. 4 ESV).

This is also a great sin that changes the shepherd to a lord, "to fend for himself." And this one can do without directly ruling with force and harshness. It is enough if one forgets that one has been sent out for the sake of others, that it was them one should take care of, feed, and live for. Instead one lives in order to provide for themselves and their own, to fill his life with works and content, to realize their own ambitions that can be very respectable and render a good reputation also in church circles. One lifts with good conscience his reward, his approved salary; one looks at his parsonage redevelopment and cultivates his interests: theology, literature, vacations, music, or photography. But he does not feed the sheep. One does not seek the lost. And so comes the Lord's word:

"The weak you have not strengthened, the sick you have not healed, the injured you have not bound up, the strayed you have not brought back, the lost you have not sought, and with force and harshness you have ruled them" (Ezek. 34:4 ESV).

Well, the last is at least uncommon in our days. It is more common with a kindness that shuns all conflicts. It shows itself also when it applies to proclaiming Law and Gospel unabbreviated. There is an inoffensiveness from the pulpit that swaddles the Word's harshness in unrefined wool and leaches out all the salt from the text before it is laid out before the congregation. That which would be life's bread becomes instead like the pure white American wheat bread, that is so finely ground and sifted, so soft and insubstantial, that it feels like cotton balls in the mouth. People despise such sermons. They show it by not bothering to hear it. A true sermon can wake anger and protests. But it engages men. And so they can begin to detect that the pastor actually preaches in this manner because he seeks their best and not his own.

He also appears as a lord who has put himself in the center. Even if he fends for himself in an inoffensive and urbane manner that in no way looks domineering, so he still belongs to the lords, to them who live according to the world's prescription, and attempts to obtain his good so long as it goes. It is to be a shepherd "for the sake of sordid gain"—even if the sordid gain manages to win his life in a very well-mannered way. It is contrary to Christ's manner of looking at people. "When he saw the crowds, he had compassion for them because they were harassed and helpless, like sheep without a shepherd" (Matt. 9:36 ESV).

Paul can teach us what it means to live for the flock and not for yourself. "I coveted no one's silver or gold or apparel. You yourselves know that these hands ministered to my necessities and to those who were with me" (Acts 20:33–34 ESV). We know that Christ has commanded that they who preach the Gospel also shall make their living from the Gospel. The laborer is worth his wages and can acknowledge it with good conscience. But the wages and all that one allows for shall give us the possibility to serve and to be shepherds for God's flock. It is not the flock and the churchly work that shall give us the possibility of living a somewhat carefree life, fulfilled by all our diverse private interests. This is the crucial line between shepherds and lords. The lords are those who come in the end to fend for themselves (Ezek. 34:2). They are thieves who come to steel, murder, and destroy, those who misappropriate the flock who have confided in them and let it be a source of income, a basis for a decent, possibly pleasant existence, and an esteemed position in this world.

When it comes to playing lord, the methods are different in our day than they were in biblical times. This can deceive us into believing that we are free of the danger. Power is not carried out in the same manner as before. Before it laid in the hands of individuals, often a few. Now the power lies in many, and we know that it is better that way. But even through the collective, one can conduct himself as lord. I have often talked about the trade union's justification. They are a part of our day's legal system, the apparatus through which we in our time come to agreement on rights and pay and balanced rights and obligations. In and of themselves, they are something good. They belong to what Scripture calls the powers, as we often say, social order. It happens that Scripture has respect for this. It comes from God; it is a piece of His care for us men.

But just as the powers in the old society could misuse their power to play lord, so can the new power in a collective be misused in the same way too. It can happen through self-interest group politics. I'm not here to speak on these thoughts. I only remind that there are responsibilities that go along with being a member of SPF and SACO. But I will point out a highly personal manner of playing lord within a framework for coming to agreement. One monitors his contractual rights in a manner that shows that he is not a true shepherd who has come to serve. To the outside it can work according to nuances: one is careful concerning his rights, watches over his free time, does not take any joy in what the service distribution prescribes, keeps track of his days off, and so on. In themselves every modern remuneration system is a temptation as one begins to see his rights and the old Adam has a sharp eye for the possibilities that are open to him. Of course there is nothing really wrong about this, except for one thing that is worst of all for a shepherd: to fend for himself and not the flock. If one fends for the flock, then he withdraws interests in his own rights. One has that to think upon; one has his attention and his thoughts on other things and does not have time to keep up on some upcoming holiday or some small medical bill. The ideal order in God's Church in the modern contractual time is on the one hand to have a good negotiator who watches over reasonable and fair wage agreements, accurate official cashiers who make sure the system works accurately, and on the other side pastors who labor and work without having time or desire to trouble themselves with small things. We pastors have every reason to be thankful that there is a system that while ensuring us a fair wage frees us from the trouble and temptation to watch over our rights ourselves. We shall not begin to look at the paragraphs to extract from them all the possibilities that can be accorded us. Also it can be a manner to fatten oneself off the food of the flock, rather than watching over it and leading it.

But now we go over to the other side of the rubrics. What does it mean to be a shepherd in contrast to lord? To lead without lording it over them?

We Are Shepherds and Teachers

Teacher, rabbi, this is what Jesus was called, and it remained a title of honor in the Early Church. It was the shepherd's duty to instruct in sound doctrine. The pastor is teacher. He has something to say, something to teach, a message that is not his own. The authority the pastor has lies in the message. It comes from God. He has the command to say it. He who understands whose message it is, he understands that it is wholly in his order when the author of Hebrews says, "Obey your leaders and submit to them, for they are keeping watch over your souls" (13:17 ESV). Here it is not a question of obedience to men but to God. Therefore, the teachers may demand nothing themselves. If people don't listen, he has no power over them. He cannot command them to do what he says. He stands there apparently powerless as the prophets and Savior did.

A true pastor can certainly be something of an authority for his congregation; he can be that as teacher who manages the Word. He can also be that in worldly things. There is so much of this in congregational work: building questions, residence questions, questions about archives and administration, about levies and personnel. Here the pastor must see the difference. In external things he is a member in a democratic society. He has the right to voice his opinion, but he shall take defeat as a "good loser" and loyally bow to the results that have gone against him. Here the rules of democratic play apply and he shall follow them, not only the enforced ones but with just the view of the worldly order that the Bible teaches us: "Be subject for the Lord's sake to every human institution, whether it be to the emperor as supreme" (1 Pet. 2:13 ESV). It is another thing when it comes to matters of faith. Here he may not bow himself to the majority—not because he is lord, "not as if we were lords over your faith." That is Christ alone, the Word alone. Neither pastor nor layman have an ounce of power or authority in matters of faith. Here we all stand under God's Word. When it comes to being a shepherd and teacher, then that pastor does not take orders from men. In this way he is a servant to his parishioners. The false shepherds, thieves who come to steal and destroy, tend to be compliant in matters of faith just to open the way for themselves into the sheep, namely the wrong way that leads to benefits and success, instead of service and self-giving.

Also, the shepherd is teacher. The shepherd shall show the way. He shall know it, and he shall follow it. But if his flock will not follow him, he has no means of forcing and driving them other than the spiritual, those which lie in the Word's own inner living power to warn and persuade. And when it comes to the congregation's external concerns, he has no more power than that which follows the law and constitution in our democratic society.

The Shepherd Is a Shepherd and Caretaker of Souls

The shepherd is a shepherd and caretaker of souls. So Jesus is called the Overshepherd, but it also applies to the shepherds He sends. They have God's flock in their care, and they shall watch over it and care for it. As caretaker of souls, the pastor has power, namely, the full power he has received from his Lord to loose and bind. The power is not really his, but the Lord's. He can do nothing other than what his Lord has given him full authority to do. He cannot operate in conflict with God's Law and promises. But when he speaks in accord with his Lord's Word, then it is loosed in heaven as he looses here on earth. But on the other hand it is a matter of pure spiritual power. If one will not follow his counsel, will not repent after his admonishments, will not believe his word, then he has no external authority to force them. And he may beware of blending the spiritual power he really has with the worldly authority he is clothed with, or maybe not. Neither may he in soul care make himself into a lord so that he spares the Gospel if men stand as his opponents in something that lies close to his heart, for example the parsonage. One can spare the Gospel when one recognizes his wrong, one can let the exchange scourge the sins one thinks he sees in his antagonist. It is just as bad to be silent about the wrongs that are common among his friends. In all soul care, the shepherd shall only see the individual souls for which the Good Shepherd has given his life. He must attempt to look on them as the Savior does so that he commiserates over them. If the pastor is bitter and sharp, so the parishioners become like sheep without a shepherd. If the pastor means to encounter his opponents in the congregation's small conflicts and bring up old grudges even when he should speak of God's ways, then they lose trust in him. He seems not to be able to forget that he didn't get what he wanted. It is also a manner of dealing as a lord and not a shepherd. But when they notice that the pastor is prepared to claim all, only that he may come with God's Word and that he swallows personal assaults and is just as normal as before, also to them who voted against him or behaved stupidly at the church council, then they become more willing to listen when he speaks as a shepherd and caretaker of souls.

When the Savior reminded the disciples of how it is among the world's gracious lords, who let people know their authority, then He added, "But it shall not be so among you. But whoever would be great among you must be your servant, and whoever would be first among you must be slave of all" (Mark 10:43–44 ESV).

There we have the final description in this same office that we are clothed with, equipped with the greatest power there is, that which lies in God's Word, a talisman for God Himself, and at the same time everyone's servant, who receives all this in our hand only to be in the service of others.

"Not domineering over those in your charge, but being examples to the flock. And when the chief Shepherd appears, you will receive the unfading crown of glory" (1 Pet. 5:3–4 ESV).

An Unfading Crown of Glory?

How many pastoral crowns of glory have faded in the course of the years! They are like an old doctor's cloak that becomes dusty, yellow, and stiff and begins to fall apart. Possibly it was the young priest's first coat, won in his first congregation, those he met with youthful charm and freshness and who met him with a near enthusiastic love. Maybe it was a crown of glory for many years, when he in his best years built up a congregation that he since replaced with another, there he will begin the same work from the beginning, only with greater experience and maturity, but where everything is different, full of disappointments, and opposition. When the old pastor looks back on his life, perhaps he sees nothing but such withered crowns of glory that he won in un-understanding and once thought he'd see around his forehead. All has withered away, and now he expects with trembling the judgment that must come when he steps before the Chief Shepherd.

But the wonderful thing is that when the Chief Shepherd comes, He does not ask about any other crown of glory than that which He Himself has with Him and only He can give. All the stores we can earn mean nothing here. Maybe it was the meaning that all would wither away and fall apart. But it manifests itself in what it seemed to be a wretched unsuccessful pastor who never completed what he wanted to do and once dreamed of. He steps forward and receives the laurel wreath, not because he did something that was noticeable in the eyes of men, but because he was one of the small servants, a shepherd and an example for the flock just in the manner that He could not be without his Savior. Maybe he thought he was the last, but he was in the biblical manner, as a servant to all.

And the Chief Shepherd kept His promises and gave him the crown of glory that never fades.

THE BIBLE'S VIEW AND THE VIEW OF THE BIBLE

Visby, 1970 and Gothenburg's Pastoral Conference, 1970

Can one say that the Bible has its own view of what we call the "view of the Bible"?

One can.

The New Testament is stamped with a very peculiar way of looking at that which we call "Scripture" or the "Scriptures", even our Old Testament. In any case, we are in a position to say how the New Testament looks at Israel's Holy Scripture. And there it is very important that we know this. First of all, we have Jesus' view of "Scripture." No one can say that this is something peripheral and irrelevant. On the other hand, it applies to the view of the Old Testament. Neither can one say that the valuation of the biblical word we encounter here might be applied to Jesus' own words but is not possible for the whole Bible.

What Is the Bible's View of Itself If We Listen to Jesus Himself?

"O foolish ones, and slow of heart to believe all that the prophets have spoken!" (Luke 24:25 ESV)

We are reminded of Jesus' word to the two disciples on the road to Emmaus. They had vented the disappointment of their hearts. They could not fathom what had happened in Jerusalem. And now Jesus tells them that what happened was just what God had already said would happen beforehand. It was determined that the Messiah must suffer all this in order to enter His glory. And what God had determined in His counsel, this He had also told His people in advance. He had given them the promise and let the Scriptures witness to His plan and intentions. And so on the way, Jesus began to go through Moses and all the prophets and explained to them what was said about Him in all of Scripture.

The Scriptures also witness about Christ. The whole of the history that they tell of point forward to Him. They are filled everywhere with types and allusions, promises and prophecies. Therefore, the Old Testament's Scriptures are something that need to be "fulfilled." This is the chief thought in all the New Testament from the Gospel of Matthew to Revelation: the Scriptures must be fulfilled in full. And this fulfillment happens through Jesus Christ. Therefore one cannot understand the Old Testament other than in light of Christ. It was a part of Jesus' work that gives explanation to the Scriptures. He didn't just do this on the way to Emmaus. Luke says at the end of his Gospel that after the resurrection He instructed His disciples precisely about this "that everything written about me in the Law of Moses and the Prophets and the Psalms must be fulfilled" (Luke 24:44 ESV). Thereafter, it says He opened their minds so that they could understand the Scriptures.

We come across the same thought again in Paul. When the old covenant's Scripture is read, there is a veil that hangs over their hearts who listen to how Moses is read. Only in Christ does it disappear. When one converts to the Lord, the veil is taken away, and then one can understand the Scripture's real meaning.

Hebrews says the same: the Law contains a shadow of the good to come, but it does not produce the thing in its real form [its true gestalt]. But Christ has come as the chief priest for the good we now possess and shows us the true meaning, for example, of the sacrificial service, the great day of atonement, and the story of Melchelzidek.

Therefore Jesus can say that it is the Old Testament Scriptures that witness to Him. "But these are they that speak of Me" (John 5:39).

Therefore even the New Testament Scriptures are penetrated by the conviction that all this that was written so long ago was written for our sake. It pointed to the future. It had a content that the people of the time could never completely understand. Only now that we live in the times of fulfillment can we conceive of the full content of what God had laid down in Scripture.

Perhaps these short hints already suffice to explain what a gulf there is between the Bible's view and the most popular view, which in our day is called "The Historical View of the Bible."

One Can Mean Many Things by "The Historical View of the Bible"

In everyday language, people most often mean by "The Historical View of the Bible" that the Bible has come into being in precisely the same way as all other books. Its authors were children of their time. They wrote and spoke as men did in their time. For unbelief and atheism, this view is obvious. One doesn't account for God. He does not exist, nor can He intervene in history. It is the conclusion that the Bible is not able to be God's Word.

Even people who say they believe in God and in a certain manner are Christians often mean the same thing when they say that they have a Historical View. They actually do believe God exists and that people can have religious experiences. But everyone has his own way of experiencing God. And when we attempt to speak about Him, it is only weak human attempts to express what is essentially inexpressible. So then the Bible's authors made human attempts to express their encounters with God in their own way. One can listen to them in the same manner that one can listen to the thoughts of good friends. Jesus is in a class of His own, but it is infinitely difficult to know what He has said, because His Word was mediated to us through simple men who shared the delusions of their times. To have a Historical View of the Bible, therefore, means to view it with the help of better knowledge, which one assumes we modern men own, so as to criticize and sift out that which we do not believe to be true.

"The Historical View of the Bible" in Swedish Theology

Now, however, the concept of the Historical View of the Bible often has a different meaning in Swedish theology. It means that God's revelation happens in history, primarily through events in which God has intervened in the world; God elected Israel, liberated them from Egypt, gave them their Law, sent their prophets and in the fullness of time His Son. A word of interpretation also belongs to these acts of salvation. The prophets and Jesus have spoken to men. These words are a part of the revelation, one of the manners in which God has intervened in the world.

This is not primarily a view of the Bible but a view of God. God is the living God, He who intervenes and operates in history. So far it is all good.

The critical point now is the view of the Bible. What meaning does one assign to the biblical Word? Here there is a whole range of conceptions in our time. On the one hand there are those who really only see God's action in the events of history and the Word as something once spoken. And now God's interventions are finished. The process through which these events have been distinguished and this Word has been entrusted to us is purely human. Therefore, the Bible is full of mistakes, and our knowledge of these deeds and works are very poor in many parts.

In other nuances of the same basic view, one allots the written documents greater value. One means that in large part they give us a correct picture of these deeds of God in history, but the basic view itself remains. The standpoint is summarized so: In our meaning the Historical View of the Bible takes into account that God speaks in concrete events of history through His ambassadors. But this message has been mediated to us through a complicated handing down, editing, and process of interpretation that is available for historical criticism.

The Gulf between the Modern "Historical View" and the Bible's Own View

If one wants to compare the Historical View of the Bible's standpoint to that of classical Lutheran teaching of inspiration, one says that the Historical View of the Bible in this meaning cannot account for any inspiration when they wrote it down. The words that once were spoken can have come from God, but the mediation of them is a human process. Therefore, there are numerous sources of error here that we can examine with normal empirical and worldly means.

It is here that the gulf between the modern Historical View of the Bible and the Bible's own view widens. For Jesus, for the apostles, and for the whole of the Early Church, an outstanding feature of the wording of Scripture has a different meaning. The whole of their manner of reading and citing shows that they are convinced that God has allowed these words to be written in just this manner so that they could be a proclamation of Christ. This meaning has long been hidden. The contemporaries of the authors could not see it, at least not clearly. But in the light of Jesus Christ, these places find their right interpretation and are understandable. This means that God Himself has shaped the process through which the Scriptures received the shape in which they speak to us. The process itself belongs to God's work in history.

It seems obvious that Lutheranism's classical doctrine of inspiration, which recognizes that the Holy Spirit gave the authors of the Bible what they would write, gives better expression to the New Testament's view of Scripture than the Historical View of the Bible.

How the Holy Spirit influenced the Bible's authors, the Christian Church has never defined. In the time of orthodoxy, certain theologians thought that the process was approximately a dictation. We might rather express the manner so: that God has linked the whole long history through which this Scripture has come to be. This applies to the oral narration, the authorship, the editing, and the selection and canon formation. So the Bible has received the shape that it should have, so that in its completeness it would carry God's message to all people in all times if read in the right manner.

We are also conscious that the Bible has its own history of origin, where men in every city are contributing. This history of origin can naturally be investigated in the same manner as any other historical event. Naturally a researcher has the right to approach the books of the Bible with the same questions that a researcher asks in such circumstances: questions of authorship, dating, source writings, linguistic peculiarities, historical veracity, and many other things. It must always have its worth for us to know what the times were like when these Scriptures were written, what the different concepts and thought processes meant for the people of the time and more. But one such analyses of the text can never give us the final answer in the question of their message, that the message really comes from God. If the New Testament is correct, one cannot understand the message simply by letting the texts be illustrated from contemporary events and notions. They must to the contrary be illustrated from Jesus Christ. Only in Him have we found its completion, which also reveals their deepest meaning. The exegetes can endlessly discuss who is really meant by the Lord's Suffering Servant in the fifty-third chapter of Isaiah. They can come up with diverse theories concerning Melchizedek. They can make it probable that some of the Psalter's most known Christocentric Psalms originally concern an Israeli king. Nevertheless, the New Testament sees in all this one of God's given types of Christ and a part of the Christian proclamation that God intentionally shaped in this manner to help us understand who Jesus was and what happened to Him. It is this New Testament's view of the Bible that we confess when we in our church on a true holy day, Annunciation Day, Good Friday, Epiphany, Midsummer, read Old Testament texts that would hardly have any connection with the day's theme if one understood them the way the research maintains is likely they were understood when they were written. If one, therefore, has the New Testament's view that these texts must be read and understood in light of Jesus Christ, then they have their given and well-motivated place in these days.

But thereby one has also said that God, already at their origin laid a meaning in them that would be revealed only in the fullness of time. Thereby one has also said that the Holy Spirit has been operative when these texts were conceived as we now have them.

If we attempt in contemporary speech to express the New Testament's view of Scripture, then I find no better formulation than this: "The Scriptures are such as God has willed that they should be." If I am not mistaken, this formulation was coined on the West Coast fifty years ago when the fight over biblical authority was hot. The first author by which I found it, I. D. Wallerius, adds that he would like to place a period there, and so not have need of some closer definition. He means that this is biblical and clear, and it is accurate. The Scriptures are such as God has willed them to be. It is tacitly understood as obvious what God's intention was: to speak to all people and all times about their salvation.

The Scriptures also have a particular purpose. They may speak through historical narratives, through poems, philosophical essays, letters, or prophecies. This purpose is to witness to salvation through Jesus Christ of the way to God through Him and of the life that one lives in His communion. The Scriptures therefore have a center from which all must be understood. Our fathers knew this well. Christ is the kernel and star of Scripture. The promise and preparation separates itself from the fulfillment. There is no question of a development where we men gradually develop our inner powers and make ourselves right representatives of God. It is, instead, God who step by step develops His plan and His meaning. He is the same in the Old Testament as in the New, but in the time of the Old Testament the most important is still partially withheld. He is there as the promise, the insinuation, and the types.

The Bible Has Been Given with a Particular Purpose and Must Be Read in a Particular Manner

That the Bible has been given to us with a particular purpose also means that it must be read in a particular manner if we will make any use of it. Because the Word deals with God's salvation, it is in essence Law and Gospel. It speaks about God's demands and God's gifts. There lies an endless wisdom in the simple word that we on the West Coast so enjoyably use: the Bible shall be read in the intention of salvation. If one wants to hear God speak in the Bible, one must ask about Him and His salvation. If one does not do this but comes with completely different questions, one cannot demand that God shall speak. The unconverted curiosity has no worth with God's Word. It has been so in all times, also in the epochs of Church history when it was obvious for all that Scripture was God's Word. It has always been a *theologia irrigenitorum*, an unconverted theology. To this also belongs the misuse of Scripture that occurred also in the old days, when one sometimes read it as a profane encyclopedia without asking about God Himself. The unconverted man can be curious and inquisitive of the Bible, but he is wary of letting it burn with fire from the Lord that condemns and forgives. He will instead search for cool, neutral, and safe facts about events and relationships that have freed themselves from any connection with salvation. Then one does not search Scripture for real theology that always deals with God and our relationship to Him but instead searches for geology, cosmology, archeology, zoology, and many other kinds of human knowledge. But the Bible was not sent out into the world for that.

Such misuse always carries its own punishment. One of the dangerous consequences was an unfruitful fight with science on points where Christianity had no reason to fight. When science began to question the accuracy of some points concerning human knowledge that one had made for himself by using the Bible as it should not be used, one felt forced to take up a fight that had little to do with faith in Christ.

If one reads the Bible with the intention of salvation and uses that for what it should be used, it functions completely as we see that it functions in the New Testament. It becomes, as Paul says, "profitable for teaching [namely about Christ], for reproof, for correction, and for training in righteousness" (2 Tim. 3:16 ESV). Everything falls in place. God may say what He wants to say in His Word. And when one in this way receives the Word as God's Word, so it becomes as Paul also says, "The word of God, which is at work in you believers" (1 Thess. 2:13 ESV). This also belongs to the essence of Scripture's inspiration. Because the Word is "thoroughly inspired" by God, it can be a living, operable Word that is a tool of the Holy Spirit. It is a means of grace. Just as the scribes in the New Testament, despite all their knowledge of the Bible and their firm faith in the Word, could not understand it because they would not receive Scripture's real message about justification by faith from God, neither can a man in our day understand that which is written in God's Word if he does not have this personal, living contact with the Spirit in the Word. And the Spirit is, we do well to note, not our own spirit that gives us inspiration or wisdom that perhaps exceeds the Word or actually gives us inspiration to criticize the Scripture. But the Spirit lives in the Word. It is what makes the Word alive. It is just this that Jesus says is the Spirit's only task: to witness about Him and remind people of what He said.

For us Lutherans, it has always been a matter of the heart to emphasize Scripture's task in the world: to witness about Christ. If one understands this, then everything in Scripture functions correctly. This is where we Lutherans distinguish ourselves from the reformed. They read the Scripture like a law book, in a different manner than we, without seeing everything in the light of Christ. That is why they preserve the Old Testament's forbidding of pictures as the Second Commandment in the Decalogue. That is why they have always attempted to apply the law as God gave to Israel to our own society in an extension that is foreign to us. The difference has very deep-going consequences for both the Divine Service and everyday life. It is for this reason that it can be so hard for a Lutheran to feel at home in a reformed church.

Even among confessional Lutherans, there can be profound nuances in conception. But they do not depend on the essentials. That which is essential and common is the conviction that the Bible is such as God has willed that it should be. We also receive it as a message from God. But when one listens to a message and reads Scripture, one must always keep the Word's value clear. One must know what form the author has chosen for his message. One listens in one way to a protocol and in a different way to a poem. A narration can have something infinitely important to say without thereby reporting a factual event. When we listen to the story of the merciful Samaritan, we don't ask for a name or year. A historical distinction can be consciously sketchy, concentrated upon the essential. There always comes to be found different meanings about how one shall understand certain parts of God's Word, if they are conceived as parables, as poems, or as history, and to what extent this history, in any case, might be stylized, sketchy, or concentrated on the essential and drawn in a shortened perspective.

But wherever God speaks in one manner or another, the message is the same. And it can be understood by whoever will receive it in its intention of salvation.

The crucial distinction between different ways of seeing the Bible consists of the answer to this question: do we believe that there is a God who speaks to us here and that He has something to say to us through these words, or do we not believe it? Are we prepared to receive this message and correct ourselves according to it, or not?

Here the ways diverge. If we separate the New Testament view of Scripture, that which has been confessed by the universal Christian Church in all times, then we are convinced that we have found something here that men cannot change but is given for all times. To this conception stands the contrary, out of which a historical outlook relativizes the Bible's message. One can concede that Jesus or the apostles actually mean or say one thing, but one dismisses it as time-bound and overcome. This can apply to the historical perspective of the world, this world's course, and the return of Christ. It can apply to marriage and the sexual life. It can apply to the division of tasks between man and woman that the New Testament says shall apply in God's congregation. There are new questions constantly arising that are asked of us Christians about the choice between the Bible's way of seeing and another that lies more in line with the way of thought in a secular world. How we choose in the end depends on our attitude toward the Word. It exposes whether we share the Bible's view or have some other view.

For us who want to hold fast to God's Word, it is always a conscious question, if we also do it in our own life—if we do it when the New Testament speaks of suffering and persecution as a natural thing, if there is not something to be surprised or embittered about? Do we do it when it means taking up our cross and not living for ourselves comfortably, not giving into ourselves in little everyday tests of patience and annoyances? Do we do it when it comes to not passing by the man who has been beaten and wounded by life's hard knocks?

The Bible's own view shall apply. Not only its view of the Word, but also its view of the cross, discipleship, love, and service. God help us all.

TO BELIEVE AS THE APOSTLES

To be a Christian is to believe as the apostles. This is not the only definition. Maybe, it's not the most important either. But it says something that inevitably belongs to Christendom.

This really needs to be said today. We have all heard this argument: "Yes, Paul says that! But Paul was, of course, just a man!" He who says this does not believe in Jesus. Or in order to say this a bit clearer, he has never understood Jesus nor his New Testament, if he has ever bothered to read it.

Jesus was not, as the liberal and biblically critical theologians say, a religious genius, who wandered around and spoke thoughtful words, which, unfortunately, were partially corrupted later on by misunderstanding people. No, Jesus was God's Son, who in the fulfillment of time became man. He is and remains "the founder and perfecter of our faith," who has something to say to all coming generations. He has provided for this Word to reach us uncorrupted. There is a Bible verse that needs to be repeated time and again in our day. I mean the words that Jesus says in John 16:12–13 sometime before His death: "I still have many things to say to you, but you cannot bear them now. When the Spirit of truth comes, he will guide you into all the truth, for he will not speak on his own authority, but whatever he hears he will speak, and he will declare to you the things that are to come" (John 16:12–13 ESV).

There is also much that Jesus could not say while He lived, much that belongs to His message and is important to hear. The apostles were not yet ready to hear it. Therefore, Jesus promised to send them the Spirit of truth, who would guide them into all the truth. He would tell them what Jesus was not yet able to say.

This is the Christian faith

We believe that Christ kept His promise to His apostles. He guided them correctly and did not err. This is common to the Christian confession.

This is what it means in our confession of faith (the Nicene) that we believe in a holy, catholic, and apostolic Church, and this faith is biblical. The Church—us too!—is built on the foundation of the apostles and prophets, where Jesus Himself is the cornerstone (Eph. 2:20). He has laid the foundation, once and for all, a foundation that can never be removed. It was laid by Christ through His Spirit, and with the apostles as tools. Therefore, the apostles had an obvious authority in the Early Church. They spoke about the ways of Christ. The sum of what they said is called in the New Testament paradosis, a word that is translated "doctrinal tradition," or something like that. This paradosis consists of direct words from Jesus and recordings of His deeds, but also of the apostolic interpretation of what Jesus did: that He died and rose again and took His place at the right hand of the Father. Later, the apostles in the power of the Holy Spirit's authority could give the congregations direction about what is permitted by particular words of Jesus, within the authority of their apostolic duty, in Christ's name, and in His ways. All this was paradosis, the teaching of the apostles.

It is this that one should hold fast to if one wants to be a Christian. The Bible says it again and again. We have in Acts 2:42 a classic sentence that tells us what we should hold fast to. The first that is mentioned there is "the teaching of the apostles." This is the foundation for all of Christendom. It emphasizes this again and again. In the letters to Timothy and Titus we see how the apostolic heritage has been handed down to the next generation. It is called a *partheke*, an entrusting of God's "good deposit entrusted to you" (2 Tim. 1:14 ESV). It shall be entrusted "to faithful men who will be able to teach others also" (2 Tim. 2:2 ESV). He who would instruct shall "hold firm to the trustworthy word as taught, so that he may be able to give instruction in sound doctrine and also to rebuke those who contradict it" (Titus 1:9 ESV).

But what if one doesn't do this? How one is then to react is taught to us in the first chapter of Galatians. He who teaches something different than the apostles is anathema. That is, he stands under the judgment of God. One cannot go unpunished for changing the teaching of the apostles.

This is highly offensive to our modern way of thinking. "That people can be so self sure!" Now it is certain and true that God does not want us to be self-confident, but this is not a question about being sure of oneself. The apostles knew whose errand they received. They had received a commission. They were led by the Holy Spirit, whom Christ had promised, in a manner that no one else can count on. They were not just common men. They were Christ's tools, called to carry out a work without counterpart, a work that would have meaning for the rest of time.

We Christians also believe in a divine revelation within historical reality. God has spoken and operated and given us something firm to hold onto. This is one of the points where Christian faith radically separates itself from modern secular thinking. This thinking has as its beloved dogma that all things are relative. It recognizes no standing truths, at least not any given to us by God. Therefore, there arises a conflict between the biblical revelation that lays claim to say something decisive, something that applies to all generations, and skeptical relativism, which says that all humanity is subject to a perpetual changing. Everything changes (flies), the ancient Greeks already said. Today it is said: everything is relative. Our customs and moral reasoning change, just look at history! Must then Christendom also adjust itself and follow the development?

Here there is a conflict, which we shall not shut our eyes to. How we stand in this conflict actually decides how we stand before Christ and Christendom.

One can attempt to escape the conflict and try to be at once a Christian and relativist through an old and tested method, which we can call the method of reductionism.

This consists of one attempting to cut away the parts of the revelation that conflict the hardest with the current thoughts of one's own day. One also considers ethics to be "dated" in certain parts of the revelation and declares that other parts are worthy of remaining.

This method has been used for so long that it has unveiled itself. It is perpetually giving different results, and this shows how arbitrary it is. It is really so that everything in the Bible can be called "dated." The revelation has, of course, occurred in time, among living men of a certain century. Therefore, it uses that time as a means of expression and concepts. Otherwise it would not have been intelligible for the people of that time. One can also stick ethics with the label "dated" wherever one wants to in the Bible. And it is wholly apparent what then determines the choice. One declares "dated" that which clashes with the established opinions in one's own time. One is himself formed by his time and its manner of thinking, and he accordingly rejects certain parts of the biblical revelation based on this. And that which is honored with the label "enduring" is that which passes for right today and is current among the people of our day. It can be common religious gods, who tolerably remain the same in every age. It can also be thoughts or concepts, which become honorable words at certain times. It can be a philosophical system such as Existentialism or Marxism. It can be humanitarian ideals such as human kindness or equality. If one hits upon something in the Bible that seems to pass for this pattern, he says: this is essential. Here lies the real point of issue in the Gospel. Here we have the capability of the future, that which has the joy of life in it! But it is precisely in this manner that one changes the eternal Gospel into something "dated," and this shows itself in the next generation, when yesterday's slogan loses its spell.

All that is essential in the New Testament can be called "dated." This applies to the Messiah, the Son of Man, the kingdom of God, redemption, the resurrection, the ascension, the second coming of Christ, and the promise of a new heaven and a new earth. One could say of all this, "So thought people in that day." But it is neither less true nor less important because of it. The revelation is no less true because God gave it to us with words and thoughts that were there two or three thousand years ago. It is no less true because it agrees with the forms of thought and valuations that are commonly accepted today. And it is not truer if it does account for them. The revelation stands on its own. The eternal in Christendom is precisely the biblical revelation, such as it is in its completeness, with Christ at the center, the message that the apostles brought out into the world.

We must also be on our watch if people say, "But that is, of course, obvious!"

We know how common it is for one to think about religious issues just as unrestrainedly as one thinks about questions of taste or politics. But what this now means—women pastors or something else—one cannot bear to think if one wants to be a Christian. When it comes to God's will, nothing is obvious but that God is right and that we, as Christians, want His will to be done. And that which is God's will we only know through the revelation, that which we possess in the Bible. When people think that something is obvious, but have not seriously asked what it is that the Bible says about the matter, so it is because they themselves have been molded by particular thoughts, which lie in time and popular opinion. They are also to a high degree "dated." But God's truth is eternal. Heaven and earth shall pass away, with all the shifting and changing thoughts of men. But My Word shall never pass away, says Jesus.

But do Jesus and the New Testament really have something to say on a question such as that of women pastors? Let us begin with what both parties are agreed upon.

This is not a question of discrimination.

With Jesus there came a new view of women, as well as children and all the different groups of people who at this time were neglected and ill-treated. All people are created by God and loved by God. He has a purpose for each and every one of them and the same disposition to them all. Jesus shocked the people of His time by His manner of treating women as equals. Among those who followed Him there was a large group of women, and they were some of His most faithful. In the Early Church, women played an active and appreciated role in the life of the congregation. Paul names women who were his coworkers again and again. We will come back to this matter.

The problem now is that the same Paul specifically says that there is a certain function in the congregation that women shall not have.

When he does this, he refers to what Jesus said. This is a fact that no Christian can overlook. One must take stock of them in one way or another. One cannot just say, "But no one thinks that way today."

What the New Testament says ought to be well-known, as lively as this debate has been. But this, in fact, is not the case. There is a single phrase that needs to be cited, and it is this that should be known: "women should be silent in the congregation." But so is it not written in the New Testament, and so this phrase as it is usually understood has no endorsement by Jesus or Paul.

There are two passages that directly refer to the question of women pastors. They are 1 Corinthians 14 and 1 Timothy 2, and they both deal with the Divine Service. It is already important to take note of this. The most detailed is 1 Corinthians 14.

Paul speaks there about the great common Divine Service, which the congregation celebrates on Sunday. One had a particular name for this Divine Service "in the gathering place." (The Greek expression is in verse 23.) They gathered all the small "house congregations," which otherwise met in the home for prayer, instruction, speaking in tongues, and prophecy. It was at the great common Divine Service, which one celebrated Holy Communion (1 Cor. 11:20). This corresponds closest to our Divine Service.

It is for this Divine Service that Paul gives directions in 1 Corinthians 14. It is not a question about some Divine Service order. He doesn't mention that which is obvious and doesn't warrant any discussion. It was these moments of Divine Service that one took over from the synagogue and that we know from other places. To this belonged the reading of Scripture, singing of psalms, and the reoccurring prayers. Neither does he mention Holy Communion. Instead, he talks about that which had not functioned as it was supposed to. These were two things. The first was the far too great a place the charismatic feature had received. He restricts them by giving them particular instructions about speaking in tongues and prophesying. In both cases he names those who may "speak" and those who shall remain quiet. The other disparity was that women had stepped up and spoken to the congregation during the common Divine Service. He says, "As in all the churches of the saints, the women should keep silent in the churches. For they are not permitted to speak, but should be in submission, as the Law also says. If there is anything they desire to learn, let them ask their husbands at home. For it is shameful for a woman to speak in church. Or was it from you that the Word of God came? Or are you the only ones it has reached? If anyone thinks that he is a prophet, or spiritual, he should acknowledge that the things I am writing to you are a command of the Lord. If anyone does not recognize this, he is not recognized" (1 Cor. 14:33–38 ESV).

Paul speaks here of "speaking" and "keeping silent" with the very same word he has used before. What this is a question of is who may step up before the congregation celebrating the Divine Service and speak to them on behalf of God. This is also not a question about disorderly chitchat. The word *lalein* that Paul uses here, is never about disorderly chitchat in the New Testament. On the contrary, it is normally used when it is God, or Jesus, or the apostles speaking to men. The best translation is often "preaching." That this is not a question of small disturbances, but about a real important matter, Paul shows with his manner of argumentation, which is so energetic and detailed that it has received a counterpart in his letter. There are four reasons he cites. First, that it is a question of an order that applies to all Christian congregations. Further, respectability demands it. Were this the only or deciding reason, we could in our days naturally institute another order. The Christian principle is of course that one conducts oneself respectably and doesn't do anything that awakens offense. But the concept of respectability changes from time to time, and we may as Christians take this into consideration. But this is not the deciding reason. Paul names two additional reasons. The one is what God's Law says. He means the Old Testament, in the consideration that it is binding also for us Christians. To this belongs the commandment to subordinate ourselves, which in the Bible means to go in under God's regulation. The New Testament has much to say about this matter. There "subordination" is one of the greatest and chief thoughts. God has firmly set in place particular and good regulations for His kingdom, regulations that a Christian joyfully subjects himself to.

The final argument, for Paul, is that this, which he writes, is a commandment from the Lord or something that Christ Himself has commanded.

To "keep silent in the churches" means then to "not speak to the congregation during the Divine Service." Paul used the same expression immediately prior for both speaking in tongues and prophesying, which neither, in this case, may "speak during the Divine Service." It is very clear what he means. And it is just as clear that one gives a misleading interpretation of Paul's words if one cites them in the false formation "The women keep silent in the congregation." This manner of formulation can actually allow for "congregation" to mean the same thing as the local congregation with all of its different working forms—or simply society, politics, and working life. But here it is a question of the Divine Service, in particular the greater Divine Service, for all the small groups to hold in common (see vv. 23 and 26). The word "ecclesia" that Paul uses here can, as you know, mean both the Church, and the local congregation and Divine Service. Here Paul speaks also about the common Divine Service, and his word cannot be stretched to apply to other actions in the congregation and in all the small meetings and gatherings that were held out in the homes. As we shall soon see—also in Paul!—a woman was allowed to both prophesy and pray among other fellow Christians.

But why does Paul then say that women ought to "ask their husbands at home"? Paul takes up a thoughtful objection: may we then not once question anything? In order to understand the meaning of this, one must know that the early Christian preaching used to be in the form of a conversation. They had learned this from the Jews. The rabbis instructed in this way, with questions and answers. By twelve years old, Jesus took His place among them and amazed all of them with His questions and answers. So He showed that He was the great teacher of Israel. "Teachers" in a Christian congregation would do this in the same manner. They laid out the Gospel through reciprocal questions and answers. In Acts we have an example of such a "conversation" (for example 20:7, 9, 11). This same word "conversation" can often be translated with "preaching." The Early Christian word for preaching (homilia) originally meant "conversation." He who asked questions during such a conversation could of course participate in the conversation and begin to function as one of the teachers. Paul had suspicions that there were such intentions among those who wanted to "ask," and therefore, he answers with a square no.

And finally Paul says that one cannot allege that the Spirit was leading them against this direction. Apparently, someone in Corinth had done this. The prophets, of course, spoke what they had been given by the Spirit. Someone who was thought to be endowed with the Spirit seems to have instructed the Corinthians to let women step up as teachers before the congregation now. Paul answers that only some really have the Spirit, and if so he must know that what Paul has written here is the Lord's command. So as Paul has said, so will Christians have it. Paul is, of course, very careful to distinguish between such questions where he knows that he has a command directly from the Lord to refer to and such where he doesn't have it (look up 1 Corinthians 7:10 and 12). Here he also knows that he has a word from the Lord, which the congregation must follow.

Therefore, Paul also makes an additional warning now, for the handling of those who will "not recognize this." In such a case, "he should not be recognized," namely by God (as good modern translations all explain, either in the text or in a note). This is the better declaration of the two readings, which one has to choose between. The other only writes, "He may be ignorant." Therefore, in such a case one may ignore him. He will answer for himself. He is blinded and it serves nothing to speak with him.

It is also revealed that for the apostle this was a meaningful issue upon which he lays the whole of his apostolic authority on the scale, in order that the Corinthians would correct themselves according to something that is an obligating order for all Christian congregations. He asks them if they really believe that they can determine the contents of God's Word. Has it gone out from them? Or are they the only possessors of it? Christendom is not something we have at our disposal and can change about. Either we take it as it is, or we can it.

This is also intelligible, that people who want to have women pastors and at the same time take their Christianity seriously in some manner must attempt to show that that which Paul says is not applicable to today.

Some say that the whole of this passage is not genuine. One would not need to waste time on this argument if it weren't for the fact that it keeps coming up again and again. So maybe we ought to look into this. This argument doesn't begin by saying that these words are lacking in some manuscript. They are present in all the manuscripts that have any significance. But in one of the four oldest and best (the earliest of them, which is called "the western text," which in many ways diverges from the other three) both verses 34 and 35 are written after 40. They can end up there by an oversight of the scribe. It can be a matter of an intentional transposition, the purpose of which one can only guess at. But according to all the rules that apply to text critics and to Bible translators the world round, the right order is the one we have in our Bible. For those who are disturbed to hear that one or another passage in the Bible is explained to be "false," it can be useful to know that there is hardly any one important passage that has not been declared to be "false" by some researcher or some group within the Church that has found it uncomfortable for his opinion. Such ill-grounded theories show only that one is not on the same wavelength as the Bible's message. It is another matter when the best manuscripts really give us reason to leave out a verse or place it within parenthesis, as happened already in our present translation from the year 1917.

There is a better argument, which is worth serious discussion, and it is the thought that this is really an issue of what one calls "a question of order."

That which Paul lays weight on would also be that the Divine Service be orderly. He has, of course, just before reminded the prophets that God is not an unorderly God. By this, one means first and foremost that it is this that is a command of the Lord. Now it is, of course, clear that "The Lord's Command" in any case first and foremost must apply to what Paul had just written about, that is women's relationship to the Divine Service. But it could, of course, be thought, that this was only a special case of the common rule: no disorder in the Divine Service. Christ wants everything "to be done decently and in order," just as Paul sums up his advice regarding speaking in tongues and prophecy at the end of the chapter.

This interpretation, however, has its difficulties. Even if a woman preached, it could, of course, have been done with good order. And wouldn't Christ have given some directions about the order for the Divine Service? Directions that touched upon speaking in tongues and prophecy? We have no trace of any such thing in the Gospels. Most important, Jesus has not given His Church any instructions for order. There was one thing that He handed down to His apostles. And in their case He prescribed something; as in the questions of Communion and marriage, His word was applied in the Early Church always as a strict obligation, even in the particulars. What Paul says here is, of course, not that the good order in the Divine Service demands that the women should keep silent, but that it is God's Law and Christ's command that demands it. That which touched upon speaking in tongues and prophesying was a question of order. There Paul gives instructions as an apostle could do. But when he comes to the question of the women's role, he takes to the argument with a completely different weight; the argument that he clearly says has unavoidable validity.

That Jesus would have given some commandment that touched upon order in the Divine Service is also improbable. That He, thereby, could have prescribed something of the women's function in the congregation is in no way improbable. Paul must, of course, have had something to refer himself to when he writes as he does. Jesus had a group of good and faithful women among His disciples. But he only called men to be apostles. And when it came time to choose a replacement for Judas, Peter says that he should be chosen from among "some of the men who followed us" (Acts 1:21). This could have been for purely practical reasons—such as the time was. But it could also be an expression of a particular purpose of the Lord Christ. In such a case, there ought to be evidence somewhere in the sources. And there is, of course, factual evidence, in this passage from Paul: "What I write to you is a command from the Lord."

It is also incorrect if one says that one cannot draw any conclusions from Jesus' choice of apostles because something is not obligating only because Jesus did so. Here we know not only what Jesus did, we also have His command if we now believe in His apostle. And—as we already said—we believe in Jesus, so we believe in His apostles, whom He has promised to lead with His Spirit.

It is the teaching office in the Early Church that is precisely the teacher's function in the sermon (with or without conversation) that Paul has in mind here. This is confirmed by the other passage in the New Testament that directly speaks to this matter. It is a passage in the First Letter to Timothy (2:12), where it says, "I do not permit a woman to teach or to exercise authority over a man; rather, she is to remain quiet" (ESV).

The Greek word that Paul employs here is "*didaskein*" and is used for those who step up as teachers by speaking God's Word before the congregation, in God's commission, and as Christ's ambassador. It is a word with deep roots in the Gospels. Jesus Himself is called "teacher" (*didaskolos*). In our church Bibles, this is translated "master," but it really means "teacher," namely a teacher of God's Word who speaks on God's behalf. Jesus has since given this commission to His apostles. He promised them the Spirit's help in order to accomplish it. He shall teach you all things, says Jesus in His farewell speech (John 14:26). In many verses an apostle is also called "teacher." Paul says that he is appointed "a preacher and apostle and teacher" (2 Tim. 1:11 ESV). Their commission was considered a commission from God. That means that God has appointed someone to be a teacher in the congregation (1 Cor. 12:28). Christ gave us some as pastors and teachers (Eph. 4:11).

It is not correct when one says that the time of the New Testament does have not any correspondence to our pastors. There is in any case a correspondence to their function that a pastor carries out today. There are men who carry out these functions. There are "pastors and teachers." And it is the "teaching" that Paul says is restricted to men.

To be a "pastor" and "teacher" belongs together. The pastor shall lead his flock on the right path and see that it receives its food. He does this as proclaimer of God's Word. He shall be "the faithful and wise manager, whom his master will set over his household, to give them their portion of food at the proper time," as Jesus says (Luke 12:42 ESV). A teacher in the New Testament is also a teacher in a very special meaning, and one misunderstands the whole thing if one gives it the same meaning as it has in modern English. It is obviously not speaking about normal school instruction. Neither is it a question of Christian instruction that occurs in Sunday School, study circles or Bible studies, or other situations where Christian laymen help by giving themselves and others better knowledge concerning God's Word, without thereby being the congregation's "shepherd and teacher." In Acts (18:26) we have a fine little example of such instruction in the oldest Church. A learned man had come to Ephesus by the name of Apollos, who preached burning in the Spirit. Among the listeners there was a Christian couple. They were tentmakers like Paul and were his faithful friends. He was named Aquilla and she was named Priscilla. Now, they noticed that Apollos did not know an important piece of information that belonged to the complete message of Jesus. So, they took him home with them and gave him basic instruction. And in this passage, as with a couple others, Priscilla is named first. Evidently she was the more important of the two.

She and her man had—at least later on—a little "house congregation," a group of Christians who gathered in their home. Certainly Priscilla was very glad about this, and Paul must have seen all this with great joy, as one can see from the greeting in his letter. This did not conflict in any way with the Lord's commandment.

The women in the early Christian congregations were in no way assigned to a passive and receptive roll. Among the people who Paul greets in the last chapter of Romans are eight different, more than a third, women. Six of them are praised for their contributions in missions and parish work. And in 1 Corinthians he mentions as an obvious thing that a woman can prophesy and pray (11:5). If one has chosen to see a contradiction between this and the command to "keep silent in the congregation," this shows that one has either misunderstood one passage or both of them. We have already seen that 1 Corinthians 14 touches on a forbiddance to step forward as proclaimer and teacher before the gathered congregation. What Paul says in Chapter 11, therefore, probably refers to the many small gatherings where one gathered for prayer and where there was speaking in tongues and prophecy occurring. In any case, it is certain that prophesying was not the same as preaching. Prophecy is an inspired talk, which comes directly from the Spirit. The prophets stepped forward only when the Spirit gave them a message to bring forward. They were not teachers. One did not demand of them that they would have a sermon on a particular occasion. If the Spirit didn't give them something to say, they had nothing to say. But if they received such a message, so it went for all the others. There were women who had the gift of prophecy (Acts 21:9), and they were obviously prophets, but they were not teachers in the congregation. An inspired prophecy was their "up building and encouragement and consolation" (as it says in 1 Cor. 14:3), but it was not what we call a sermon, and it was not recognized as the instruction which "the teachers" gave the congregation. On the contrary, it is mentioned next to such instruction (1 Cor. 14:6), just as the prophets are mentioned next to apostles, evangelists, and teachers. Prophecy belonged to the charismatic gifts that could fall on both men and women. It was for this reason that a woman could prophecy. At the same time, it was clear that she was not called to be "pastor and teacher." And something similar applied to prayer. When people prayed together, so as one did in the home and in the small house congregations, kind of like we do in prayer circles, a woman could obviously lead in prayer. How it was with the common chief Divine Service we do not know for sure. It is possible that a woman with the gift of prophecy in likeness to the Old Testament prophets went before all the people when God gave her a message. In any case she was allowed to do it in small gatherings.

The women at the grave are declared to have been among the first women pastors because they received a commission to "proclaim the resurrection." This is a grave misuse of the word. The women at the grave never received a commission to "proclaim." They were sent on an errand. They were to go to the apostles with the greeting that Jesus had risen and was going before them to Galilee, where they would be able to see Him. They brought His greeting and thereby had completed their commission. None of them gave a sermon; still less were they ever a pastor or teacher for a congregation. If one wants to use them for an example and model, they can exemplify the task that every Christian has to witness to what they have seen and heard. Every person, man or woman, who knows that Christ lives has a greeting to bring before the people who are close to them.

The debate about women pastors has a great potential to determine where people stand on other questions. Very often, particularly in the letters to the editor columns of the papers, it shows that they have their points of view because they do not at all believe in any of God's given revelation. They reject the whole foundation upon which Christendom is built: the apostles and prophets as foundation, Christ Himself is the cornerstone. It is very useful and clarifying to first of all try to find out if he who expresses himself in the debate believes that Jesus was God's Son, that He has given us a truth that can never change, and that He sent His apostles the Holy Spirit, which led them right and never wrong. If a person doesn't believe this, it is meaningless to discuss how the Christian Church ought to be formed.

But this question also has the capability of revealing deep underlying differences in theologies that the laymen are seldom conscious of. During this century there has been a radical school of theology that began with the so-called liberal theology around the turn of the century, whose common characteristic is that they doubt that the New Testament gives us a reliable picture of Christ and Christendom's origin. We meet here such thoughts as the Christ never wanted to start any Church, that the early congregations did not have any office, that a great deal of Paul's letters didn't have anything to do with him but came long after, possibly in the year 120. If one has such opinions, it is clear beforehand that the Church (if we now shall have any Church) can organize the office of pastor however they want (if we will now have any pastors).

In this little writing, we have left all such opinions to the side and instead tried to take from such points of view, which may be meaningful for Christians, people who believe in Jesus as God's Son as the New Testament presents Him. A Christian should be on his watch so that he doesn't borrow an argument from them in the heat of debate, which in actuality he has left biblical Christianity. If we want to be Christians, we must stand on the ground of the Bible's Word. Unfortunately, we can still have different opinions. But we can at least carry the conversation out from a common ground.

Why has Christ given us such a commandment?

This is finally a question that we cannot let be still. Essentially it is preposterous. God, of course, does not need any motivation for His decision. In the apostolic Church, it was obvious that what the Lord said could not be questioned. Yet we can still seek after connections that can deepen our understanding of the Gospel. And we have in our New Testament an indication of them at least. In Ephesians (5:21) we hear that there is a parallel between the Church and marriage. Christ is the Head in the Church; the man is the head in the family. Christ and His Church belong together. They complete a body in a union that God has created. In the same manner, God has made man and wife one. In both cases it is a question about an invisible but real union that God has established. It is upon both of these spheres that the New Testament says God wants to have an order between man and women that gives the man the role of "the head." It is well to note that this is not in the manner that the world finds natural, so that one rules in order for himself to have advantage of it. In God's kingdom all tasks and commissions mean that one is placed to serve others. "Husbands, love your wives, as Christ loved the church and gave himself up for her" (Eph. 5:25 ESV). It is not patriarchy, but such is the new life in God's kingdom. In Christ it is so that "woman is not independent of man nor man of woman" (1 Cor. 11:11 ESV). So Paul says in the same breath as he said that the man is his wife's head. It is not a contradiction. So it is in a Christian marriage, where both the spouses have Christ as their Lord. They can share all, discuss everything, and pray for guidance in everything together. And simultaneously the wife can, if the man despite everything has different opinions, in faith and love say, "Then it is as you have decided, for Christ has placed you as head. But remember your responsibility." This is not patriarchalism. It is God's way of having a good marriage function. So the New Testament teaches us. Accepting this in biblical terms is to "subordinate yourself," which means to willingly and joyfully go in under God's order as a free person without any feeling of being oppressed.

The congregation is also, according to Ephesians 5, a parallel to the marriage at home. It is God's family, where Christ is the Head, and where He has initiated His servants as proclaimers and housefathers. He who is pastor and teacher for the congregation is a housefather for the people of God's house. He is this on behalf of Christ, in the apostles' succession. Is this possibly why God wants to have a social order between women and men in His Church? That He wants it is in any case clear, if we shall believe as the apostles.

This is not patriarchalism as the New Testament determines its view of these things. The Jewish society was without a doubt patriarchal. The Hellenistic culture was also patriarchal to a great extent—though there were certain threads of what we would call women's emancipation.

Women priests were a common and accepted phenomenon. But the New Testament is not patriarchal.

Patriarchalism means an order of society where the men rule and keep check over the whole line, in work life, politics, administration, and so on. But in the New Testament, it is accepted as obvious that there were women workers as leaders in businesses, who did like Lydia from Thyatira in Acts 16:1. She was a prominent figure among the Christians in Philippi. It is only in two circumstances that the New Testament speaks of a social order between women and men, namely the home and the Church. And this happens without reference to societal order, but it represents an order that rules in God's kingdom and "in the home" also because one believes in Christ and wants to live according to His will.

It is also something that has to do with love for God. Love is often used as an argument in churchly debates, and correctly so. One may see that one does not pursue the Christendom's falsification, which can be called "conversion through a formula." It can go so that one uses a key word that one declares fits together the essentials in Christendom. One can take such a word as love, equality or freedom. One believes that one knows what the word means beforehand. One does not examine what the Scriptures have to say about the matter. Instead one uses this key word as a divination to find what belongs to a true Christendom. But this "love" one talks about is possibly a humanitarian human kindness or a common well-wishing or something else people today mean by "love." The Bible's agape is something entirely different, something new that has come into the world through Christ and is only found in operation where people live in communion with Christ. One can learn to know this love only through the Scriptures and by entering the world that the Gospel opens for us.

If this applies now to the question of women and the office, then it is natural from a secular and humanist viewpoint, and it is loveless to hinder women from being a pastor. But if one sees the matter from the Scriptures, it must be loveless to ordain a woman to the office of pastor if God does not will it. And what God wants in such a case one can only know through the revelation in Scripture.

What shall we then do?

If we will now believe as the apostles? If we will follow the Scriptures and are convinced that God knew well what would happen in Sweden in the 1900s and actually speaks to us also about this? For that is just what we Christians believe.

It is clear that God wants to have both women and men to serve Him in the Church. This applies only to draw boundaries as He wants to have them. We have not done this in the past. Much of the wealth of the Early Church with its many servants has been forgotten. The pastor has taken over almost all functions, which have come together in the human office. In our century, a change for the better has slowly happened. It has often been awakening movements and free associations that have understood to take in the women better than the Church has done. We need a warmhearted joy for women's work in the Church with a manifold of services where a woman with a call to serve God in His Church can have use of her gifts. Much has improved on this point during the last decades, but there are also tendencies to stop the good developments and to push women to become pastors. This constitutes a great wrong against the women who on reason of their Christian convictions don't want to be that. And there are, though the mass media would rather be silent on the matter, at least as many women as men who are convinced that the New Testament says to us that women are not called to be the congregation's pastor and teacher.

There is much we as Christian people can agree on even if we think differently on the question of women pastors. They can, however, agree on many points concerning the issue. They know that it is not a question of equality in the civic and social sense. They know that the misgivings do not depend upon discrimination or common reactionary manners of thinking. They know that this is a serious question, which must be answered from the Scriptures. Therefore, they can also live together in the Church. This is clear enough from experience. Those who believe that a woman pastor has her office from God use her services thankfully. They who do not believe this, dodge engaging her. And no one should be forced to do something that obviously violates his or her conviction. And then we hope and pray that God would finally lead us all in the right way as we humbly and sincerely listen to His Word and want that His will should happen.

It was 1992 or so. I was young pastor, fresh out of the seminary. I wrote to Bo Giertz and expressed my deep appreciation for The Hammer of God, which had a profound effect upon me and so many other young men, raised in the confines of pietistic and anti-catholic [small c!] corners of the LCMS. Giertz was Walther's Law and Gospel in novel form. Like Walther's classic, it captivated me. The aged Giertz kindly replied, noting that his book was based upon his own experiences as a young pastor in Sweden. While in the office, I was just beginning to comprehend the office of the ministry as a divine mandate and gift, wholly given to the task of forgiving sins. Having these ordination sermons in English is a blessing beyond compare. They breathe a graciousness and love for the church which gave us birth, yet pull us toward a pastoral love and practice among God's people flowing from Lutheranism's great gospel center. Three cheers!

Matthew C. Harrison
Assistant Pastor, Village Ladue
President, Lutheran Church-Missouri Synod

More Best Sellers from

Find these titles
and more at 1517.org/**shop**

Never Go Another Day Without Hearing the Gospel of Jesus.

Visit **www.1517.org**
for free Gospel resources.